CHRIS MCLEOD

PAT CUMMINS

COURAGE, CONTROVERSY, CONVICTION

Published by Wilkinson Publishing Pty Ltd
ACN 006 042 173
PO Box 24135, Melbourne, VIC 3001, Australia
Ph: +61 3 9654 5446
enquiries@wilkinsonpublishing.com.au
www.wilkinsonpublishing.com.au

Follow Wilkinson Publishing on social media.

WilkinsonPublishing
wilkinsonpublishinghouse
WPBooks

© Copyright Chris McLeod 2024

All rights reserved. No part of this publication may be reproduced, stored in a retrieval system or transmitted in any form by any means without the prior permission of the copyright owner. Enquiries should be made to the publisher.

Every effort has been made to ensure that this book is free from error or omissions. However, the Publisher, the Authors, the Editor or their respective employees or agents, shall not accept responsibility for injury, loss or damage occasioned to any person acting or refraining from action as a result of material in this book whether or not such injury, loss or damage is in any way due to any negligent act or omission, breach of duty or default on the part of the Publisher, the Authors, the Editor, or their respective employees or agents.

ISBN: 9781922810564
A catalogue record for this book is available from the National Library of Australia.

Cover and internal design by Jo Hunt

Printed and bound in Australia by Griffin Press, a part of Ovato

CONTENTS

INTRODUCTION	1
1. ANNUS MIRABILIS	7
2. FROM ASHES TO ASHES	18
3. A TEST OF THE BEST	35
4. ONE-DAY, SOME DAY!	44
5. TESTING TIMES	54
6. SHORT AND SWEET	63
7. G-WIZ	79
8. MORE BANG FOR THE BUCK	87
9. A COURAGEOUS DECISION	100
10. THE LONG RUN	114
11. CAN BOWL, CAN BAT, CAN FIELD	121
12. CLOSING THE 'GATE	132
13. IT'S JUST NOT CRICKET	144
14. VIEW FROM THE OUTER	156
15. THE GAP YEARS	166
16. COMETH THE MAN	177
17. PRINCIPLES AND CONSCIENCE	184
18. LOOKING AHEAD	193
19. THERE'S SOMETHING ABOUT PAT	200
20. THE CUMMINS FILE	205
21. THE CUMMINS COLLECTION	214

INTRODUCTION

"You look at their overall Test record since he's been captain, it's outstanding. And now he's a World Cup-winning captain, a World Test Championship-winning captain and a captain who retained the Ashes, so that negativity needs to be put aside now. He thoroughly deserves every plaudit that comes his way as far as leadership is concerned."

RICKY PONTING, FORMER CAPTAIN OF AUSTRALIA, 2024

The governing body of global cricket, the International Cricket Council (ICC), named Pat Cummins the Sir Garfield Sobers Cricketer of the Year for 2023.

No lesser authority than the "bible of cricket", Wisden, agreed and named him its Leading Cricketer of the World for 2023.

The personal honours were just-rewards for Cummins as he led Australia through a year of great achievement and headed into 2024 with hope of more success.

The contents of Australia's Trophy cabinet at the end of 2023 were a tribute to the team and its captain: The World Test Championship (WTC), the World Cup in One-day Internationals and the Ashes Urn that England, at home, failed to wrest from the visitors in a drawn series.

Oh, and while all that was happening, he took more Test wickets than any other fast bowler in the world.

He hasn't said so outright, but it would be high on Cummins' wish list to find a place in the trophy cabinet on his watch for the Border-Gavaskar Trophy that Australia hasn't had its hands on since the 2014-15 series at home.

A five-Test home series beginning in November 2024 would provide a good opportunity to wrest back the trophy. A five-Test series in India in 2025 would be problematic – Australia hadn't won a series there since 2004.

In 2024, Australia returned to the top of the world Test rankings. Not a bad 12 months' work, and even winning a Test match in India was considered a plus, alongside the WTC victory.

Winning the ODI World Cup was a "legacy" moment for Cummins and the Australians, particularly as it was a victory over India in India, although somehow it wasn't sufficient for Australia to overtake India at the top of the ODI rankings.

After his triumphant first series as captain, the 4-0 Ashes victory against England in Australia in 2021-22, Cummins cemented himself in the top job as someone not afraid to challenge convention – and show faith in his players.

When he won the toss and decided to bowl first in the Cricket World Cup final in 2023 against an undefeated Indian team, he knew he was going against conventional wisdom.

The match was on India's home turf, the Narendra Modi Stadium in Ahmedabad, on a pitch that historically favoured local spinners and before a crowd of around 100,000 people almost entirely decked out in blue to support the home team.

Australia emerged victorious; the masses that had confidently expected an Indian win fell silent.

Cummins and conventional wisdom don't always go together, as the late Ron Reed pointed out in the first book to chart the rise of Pat Cummins to the top job in Australian cricket, *Captain Pat: Cometh the Hour, Cummins the man*.

It was a decision against conventional wisdom that landed

INTRODUCTION

Cummins the captaincy in November 2021.

A fast bowler hadn't captained Australia in a Test since Ray Lindwall – in one Test – in 1956. Even former captains queried the move. Allan Border was adamant Cummins shouldn't do it, fearing the added burden would hurt his standing as the world's No.1 bowler.

Could Cummins handle the captaincy and still bowl those lethal 140 km/h deliveries on which Australia had become so reliant?

By 2024 Cummins had dropped to No. 5 in the ICC's Test bowling records, trailing teammate Josh Hazlewood who had risen to No. 2.

It seemed clear his bowling hadn't affected his captaincy, but was the reverse true?

After his first spell in the first Test in Brisbane on 23 November 2021 Cummins went to lunch wondering whether Allan Border may have been right.

He recalled afterwards: "That first spell was terrible. I didn't bowl particularly well. My mind was worried about field placements and other things. Then I bowled another spell, and I was fine. But it made me understand why other people thought I shouldn't take the captaincy on."

Whatever he had for lunch – or didn't have – isn't recorded but it was a more confident Pat Cummins in the second half of the day.

England finished its first innings with 147 runs on the board after deciding to bat first; Cummins had taken five wickets.

He must have felt a lot better. Australia made 425 runs (Cummins 12) in reply to set up the inevitable victory in the rain-interrupted match when England in their second "dig" could manage only 297, just enough to make Australia bat again for a few overs to get the 20 runs needed.

The captain took two wickets in England's second innings. He had seven wickets for the match and Australia had seen off England in no uncertain terms.

Cummins had answered the questions about any conflict between his leadership and bowling responsibilities.

PAT CUMMINS

He added an exclamation point a year later in Melbourne when he claimed 10 wickets against Pakistan to clinch a 3-0 series win over the visitors. It was his second career 10-fer; the first was in Brisbane against Sri Lanka in 2019, when he didn't have the responsibility of captaincy.

The Ashes win was the kind of start everyone had wished for under the new leadership team put in place in the wake of the "sandpapergate" scandal in South Africa and the later unrelated resignation of captain Tim Paine.

Ron Reed had summed up how appointing Cummins captain turned into a stroke of genius: "While nobody could predict precisely how that would play out, one thing was beyond certain – it was going to capture the imagination of the Australian public big-time; major talking points were guaranteed, the headline writers and talking heads would be earning their money double-time for the next two months. And if Australia won, so much the better – a new king of Australian cricket would have been crowned to unstinting applause.

"That's how it panned out – professional scriptwriters couldn't have improved on it, as captain Pat led from the front, took the most wickets, changed the image of the team for the better and guaranteed himself a level of fame and fortune rarely seen before in Australian cricket."

Three years later, nothing had changed that would alter the view that Cummins was the right man for the job.

After the home Ashes series in 2021, to the end of the 2023-24 summer in Australia, Cummins led his team in another 43 matches, Tests and ODIs, with considerable success. Some surprises, too.

Such was Cummins' newly-gained reputation for leadership that upon his return to the Indian Premier League in 2024 he was snapped up as captain by Sunrisers Hyderabad. He was happy to have new Australian batting hero Travis Head in his line-up.

Cummins took his team to the final of the 2024 IPL, having missed the play-offs altogether in the three previous seasons. The hope for glory unfortunately came to nothing, the team soundly beaten by the Kolkata Knight Riders.

INTRODUCTION

T20 cricket was going to sustain him through much of 2024 as Australian didn't have any long-form cricket in the diary until late in the year. After the IPL campaign he was off to the US and the West Indies for the T20 World Cup (with Mitch Marsh taking charge of the team) before joining a San Franciso-based team in America's fledgling Major League Cricket competition.

Cummins was not the "main man" in Australia's failed T20 World Cup campaign in 2024 but he produced the amazing feat of successive hat-tricks, his first and second in the 20-overs short form. He became the first bowler to pick up two hat-tricks in the same edition of the T20 World Cup, in matches against Bangladesh then Afghanistan. But his efforts weren't enough to get Australia into the semi-finals with losses to Afghanistan (by 21 runs) and India (by 24 runs).

Cummins seemed to take Australia's early departure from the competition to heart, posting on Instagram: "Not the finish we were after. Gutted to be heading home early but love this team and playing alongside these boys."

Questions arose about why, given his success in leading Australia in the ICC's World Test Championship and ODI World Cup, he wasn't captain for the T20 World Cup. He'd also led his T20 IPL team to the play-offs in India.

It was not a question he asked, of course, seemingly happy to let Mitchell Marsh carry that burden.

India went on to defeat South Africa by seven runs in the final, getting their first ICC silverware since 2013 in the superseded Champions Trophy.

It hasn't just been solely deeds on the cricket pitch that have thrust Cummins into the limelight. He has taken a stand on social issues and causes, using his profile to advantage.

He flushed out some critics, but he doesn't care about that. He stands up for what he believes, something many more people could take on board.

People, mostly those who still refer to cricket from years gone by as "the good old days," might call him Captain Woke and like names, but that kind of commentary helps him highlight the causes he holds dear. As he says, it emboldens him. And his views don't seem to particularly concern younger cricket fans as much as it does the suited gentlemen in the Members' Lounge.

Cummins also went through some tough times. His mother in Sydney became seriously ill while he was away on the tour of India in 2023. Without a second thought he rushed home to spend some time with her and the rest of the family before she died. He didn't need to explain his absence from the rest of the Test series – it was clearly the right thing to do.

That's what he always tries to do – the right thing.

It is worthwhile then in this book to look at the three years that Pat Cummins has spent in the limelight – his captaincy, his conscience and a touch of controversy.

Ron Reed foreshadowed the need for such a book in *Captain Pat* in 2021: "This won't be the last book about him, or by him, nothing surer than that."

In Ron's absence and having contributed to his efforts back then, I was happy to take up the challenge.

I don't put myself in the same class of sports writing as Ron, so where some of the points he made in *Captain Pat* remain relevant to what has happened since, I have revisited them.

But the aim here is to examine the development of Captain Pat in the years that he has been the face of Australia's reimagined cricket team.

CM

1
ANNUS MIRABILIS

You have to win a World Cup. You can't wait for it to happen. You have to be brave, take the game on. There was a big shift after the first two games. There was total buy-in and it worked. This is a year we will remember for a long time.
AUSTRALIAN CAPTAIN PAT CUMMINS ON WINNING THE WORLD CUP

Pat Cummins proved his captaincy credentials right from the start of his tenure with Ashes success on home soil in 2021-22.

Two years later, as one Indian cricket writer described it, 2023 was an "annus mirabilis" for Cummins, or as former Australian captain-turned commentator Richie Benaud might have said, a "simply marvellous year."

By the end of 2023, Cummins' captaincy record for the year looked something like that of any other captain's entire career.

The numbers spoke for themselves: across all formats, including the World Cup and warm-ups, Cummins led Australia in 33 matches for 25 wins, six losses and two draws.

Even the draws were significant; the drawn fourth Ashes Test in England kept the home team from getting its hands on the coveted "Urn," the series finishing 2-2.

Later, Cummins said he believed his team created a career-defining legacy by winning two International Cricket Council (ICC) trophies

— the World Cup for One-Day Internationals and the World Test Championship (WTC).

He was of course in the Australian team primarily as bowler, and a dangerous one at that. In 2023 his 42 wickets in Tests at an average of 27.50 were second only to Nathan Lyon's 47 wickets at an average of 24.95, the top two wicket-takers among the world's bowlers.

Cummins had an impact in ODIs as well, even if he wasn't among the top wicket-takers.

The World Cup ODI final showed what the captain was capable of. His spell of 2-34 included the game-changing wickets of Virat Kohli and Shreyas Iyer.

Batting wasn't a strength, but he was acknowledged as a key wicket in the tail-end of an innings. Even England knew that; speedster Ollie Robinson reportedly said at Edgbaston for the first Ashes Test that once Cummins had gone, there were "three No.11s" to dismiss.

Robinson may have wrongly assumed that getting past Cummins was a simple matter. It wasn't.

If he included Nathan Lyon in the threesome, he would also have been wrong.

Cummins made 38 valuable runs in the first innings, and the heroics of him and Nathan Lyon saw Australia home in a 55-runs stand for the ninth wicket to win by two wickets. Cummins was unbeaten on 44.

It was an *annus mirabilis* for Cummins and the Australians but at times it looked like it could have turned into what HRH the Queen might have said, an *annus horribilis*.

Retaining the Ashes on England soil was a sterling effort among several, Cummins revealing after the deciding match that he'd played for five days with a fractured wrist.

He was OK to bowl but batting gave him grief, making his first innings knock of 36 runs off 86 balls even more meritorious.

"It hurt day one (fielding) when I did it and it hurt a lot when I was batting, but I didn't think it was too bad," Cummins said. "Then with each day it got a little bit sorer, so I knew it was probably bone as opposed to a muscle."

The wrist was found to be fractured, and he was sidelined for the short-form series in South Africa in August-September after the Ashes. How would that affect his career as strike bowler, even as captain?

He'd had more than his fair share of injuries in his career, as is well-documented, and probably missed more than 60 Test matches and 90 ODIs since his debut in 2011.

A huge sigh of relief was heard in Australian cricket circles when he returned to the team in 2023 in time for the ODI World Cup in India. The rest, as they say in the classics, is history.

As things turned out he missed more games in 2023 through the loss of his mother than injury, misses neither he nor anyone else was concerned about at all, as family meant much more to him than cricket at that time.

The year began on home soil with a drawn third Test with South Africa; Australia already had clinched the three-Test series by winning the first two late in 2022.

It was then off to India in February for four Tests on tracks where the local spin bowlers were expected to dominate.

Australia managed to win one Test in conditions that never really suited their fast bowlers. The spinners held their own in most matches and topped the team's wicket-takers; Nathan Lyon took 22, Todd Murphy 14 and left-armer Matthew Kuhnemann 9.

Cummins played in just the two Tests before flying home to be with his family during his mother's illness; he took three wickets in the first two Tests. Michell Starc was the best of the quicks with 10-301 in the five matches.

The Border-Gavaskar Trophy went the way of India again, but Australia was to put that behind them and go on to a hectic schedule for the rest of the year.

At least they'd broken through for a win on Indian soil – 14 wins (plus a tie) from 52 Tests played tells how hard it has been to beat the

Indians at home. Australia last won a Test match in India in Pune, in 2017, and hadn't won a series there since 2004.

There were kudos for Cummins himself and he didn't go unrewarded for his year's work.

Wisden named him Leading Cricketer in the World, the first Australian in 12 years to be so honoured.

Cummins eclipsed England's Ben Stokes who had won the prestigious title three times in the last four years.

Wisden's Cricketer of the Year award is the oldest individual award in cricket and dates to 1889.

Announcing the award in April 2024, Wisden editor Lawrence Booth pointed to retaining the Ashes in England, winning the ICC World Cup for one-day cricket and the WTC as Cummins' credentials.

And, Booth added: "In 2023, no other seamer in world cricket took more than his 42 Test wickets."

The Wisden Trophy for Test performance of the year went to Australian Travis Head for his match-defining 163 in the WTC final against India at The Oval. Head was a player who really blossomed under the leadership of Cummins.

Wisden also chose its five Cricketers of the Year – an award that can only be won once in a career – and is generally based on performances in the previous English season.

Three of the 2023 awardees were Australians – Usman Khawaja, Mitchell Starc and Ashleigh Gardner – who played in men's and women's Ashes series during the year.

The ICC named Cummins as its Cricketer of the Year, an award he clearly deserved but one in which he credited his team for the success.

"It's a huge honour. It's been a big year with lots of wonderful team success," Cummins said.

"To get this individual honour is huge. Pretty amazed actually. In terms of an individual accolade, it's right up there and really special."

He singled out Travis Head's role in Australia's Test and ODI success.

"All the other nominees had fantastic years as well. Trav as a teammate…we saw him in the World Test Championship and in the World Cup final where he's man of the match in both of them," Cummins said.

"Jadeja and Kohli are both super consistent. There are games where you can't keep them out of it, they find a way to drag their team out of trouble and win it for them.

"To be alongside those guys has been really special."

The ICC named Khawaja as its Test Player of the Year.

Cummins began collecting "cricketer of the year" awards back in 2019 – ICC men's Test Cricketer of the Year. He was named in ICC men's Test Teams of the Year in 2019, 2022 and captain in 2023.

All Australia's major triumphs in 2023 were away from home. In fact, the Australians spent almost six months on the road and didn't play international cricket at home between February and December. It was a similar story for March to November in 2024.

Cummins captained Australia in 11 Test matches in 2023. The record: 11 Tests for five wins, four losses and two draws. Australia played 24 ODIs, including World Cup Matches.

The Test victories included the WTC final against India by a massive 209 runs at The Oval in England.

In white-ball cricket, The Australians with Cummins as captain in ODI internationals, lost three of their first four matches of 2023 (including the first two of the World Cup) but recovered to win nine in a row, including a record sixth World Cup for Australia.

Cummins rushed home in March, mid-way through the Test series in India to be with his mother Maria and family during an extremely sad time. His mother died while he was there, and he did not return for the remainder of the series.

The loss of his mother affected him greatly. "I think about her every day," he said after Australia won the World Cup in November.

"Cricket's been a big part of our family forever, and to see the respect and love shown from our oldest rivals, it was really special," he said when the Indian team offered its condolences and support. "She's seen a lot of successes before this year, and she's a huge part of who I am, and I'm sure she would have been really proud."

Having lost the Border-Gavaskar Trophy 2-1 in India, Australia was expected to struggle against India in the WTC in June.

But led admirably and astutely by Cummins, Australia put the No. 1 ranked team to the sword and claimed the top ranking for itself. The return of Cummins to lead the team was a huge boost.

His leadership qualities were evident throughout the year, but his individual performances were equally impressive.

The year finished with two Tests of a three-match home series against Pakistan. Australia won all three matches, including the third Test in January 2024.

By the start of 2024 Cummins' record had defied thoughts that fast bowlers couldn't be successful captains.

Australia had won a three-Test series 1-0 in their first visit to Pakistan in 24 years in March-April 2022 and hopes were high for Australian success in the return visit.

The 2023 Boxing Day Test in Melbourne at the end of the year showed Cummins still had that ability to swing a match by his own hand.

He became the first Australian in 30 years to take 10-wickets in a Boxing Day match. The last to do it was Bruce Reid, in back-to-back Boxing Day Tests in 1990 and 1991.

Captain Pat collected 5-48 in Pakistan's first innings and followed up with 5-49 in the second. His wickets included his 250th in Tests.

His first innings haul gave Australia a 54-runs lead. Late on day four, he helped initiate a collapse that saw the visitors lose five wickets for only 48 runs.

"Really happy for a few reasons," Cummins said. "The main reason is that's the best I've felt like I bowled for a little while.

"The rhythm felt really good, I felt like I had good pace, I knew where my wrist was and I could control the seam, good bouncers. I felt really happy with how I was bowling even if I wasn't taking wickets."

ANNUS MIRABILIS

The tour of India followed.

Steve Smith took over the reins when Cummins left the squad after two Tests. Family was his top priority, and everyone understood that.

Australia lost the series 2-1, winning the third Test by six wickets.

The tour ended on a positive note despite the Test series loss when Australia defeated the home side by 21 runs in the decider to clinch the three-match ODI series 2-1.

Australia's sole victory in the Border-Gavaskar Trophy was enough to secure the team's spot atop the World Test Championship rankings and a place in the looming final at The Oval.

The WTC series was played from 2021 to 2023 among the nine full members of the ICC.

Playing the final on "neutral" territory (England) in June gave Australia hope of getting some sort of revenge against India after the Border-Gavaskar result.

Cummins lost the toss and Australia was put into bat on a green-top wicket in overcast conditions. Cummins would have bowled first if he'd won the toss.

A century by Travis Head in difficult conditions paved the way for an Australian victory.

Cummins said of man-of-the-match Head: "He has been brilliant throughout the campaign. It started with the Ashes a couple of years ago. He just puts the pressure right back on the bowlers and suddenly you are thinking about how to contain runs rather than taking wickets."

Australia became the first cricketing nation to win all ICC trophies. They'd already won five 50-over World Cup trophies, two Champions Trophy titles, and a T20I trophy (2021).

All that was left was to hold the three ICC trophies at one time. The T20I World Cup was the one the Australians didn't have in the cabinet in 2023 but would get the chance in 2024.

Bazball was all the buzz in England under coach Brendon McCullum when Australia headed into the Ashes series straight after the WTC final.

The series was drawn 2-2, enough for Australia to retain the Ashes.

Cummins picked up 18 wickets in nine innings with an impressive economy rate of 4.27.

The year of Tests finished back home in Australia at the end of the year where Australia won the first two of a three-Test series against Pakistan.

Taking 10 wickets in his last match of the year, against Pakistan at the MCG in the second Test, was the icing on the Cummins cake of 2023.

He finished 2023 with 42 Test wickets in just 19 innings.

In the 2023 ODI World Cup final against India in November, Cummins picked up crucial wickets of Kohli and Shreyas while conceding just 34 runs, not giving away a single boundary.

Virat Kohli won his fourth ICC Men's ODI Cricketer of the Year award after guiding India to the Cricket World Cup final. But it was there Kohli met his match in the shape of Pat Cummins.

The wicket of Kohli in the 29th over was critical to Australia's chances. India was 3-148, looking ready to post a big score with Kohli at the crease.

The loss of Kohli seemed to spark and Indian collapse and the side was all out for 240 in their 50th over. Cummins took 2-34 in his 10 overs. Australia won the game in their 43rd over, Travis Head making 137.

Not only did Pat Cummins excel with the ball, he also contributed with the bat, particularly in the case of the preliminary World Cup game against Afghanistan, not through weight of runs but with the ability to hold up an end.

His 202 runs partnership with Glenn Maxwell became the highest eighth-wicket partnership in ODI cricket history, the first double-century partnership for a number eight pairing or lower in ODIs. Cummins was unbeaten on 12 (68 balls faced) in the eighth wicket stand while Maxwell blasted his way to 201 not out.

Australia was 7-91 when the pair came together, chasing 292.

ANNUS MIRABILIS

The numbers and milestones for Pat Cummins in 2023:
- He became the first captain to take a 10-wicket haul in a Test match in Melbourne against Pakistan and the first to take 10 wickets in a Boxing Day Test at the MCG for three decades.
- He became the first captain to take five-fers in both innings of a Boxing Day Test.
- His 10-97 against Pakistan made him the second Australian captain in Test history to achieve a 10-wicket haul. The other one was Allan Border, who took 11/96 against West Indies in 1989.
- He finished the year with 59 wickets across all formats, becoming the Australian captain with the most wickets in a calendar year, surpassing. Richie Benaud's 54 wickets in 1959.
- He took 42 Test wickets for the year, the second-most by an Australian captain in a calendar year, behind Richie Benaud's 54 in 1959. He was second to team-mate Nathan Lyon in 2023 who had 47.
- He became the only captain to win two ICC trophies in the same year (WTC 2023, ODI WC 2023).
- His tally of Test wickets reached 250, tying the record for the third-fastest Australian bowler to reach that mark, alongside Mitchell Johnson. Dennis Lillee still holds the record, in 48 matches, followed by Glenn McGrath and Shane Warne, both tied at 55 matches.
- He became the third player to win the ODI World Cup as both captain and player, joining Ricky Ponting and Michael Clarke.
- His 6-91 in the third Test against England at Leeds in 2023 was the third-best in an innings by an Ashes captain, after Monty Noble (6-52 in 1948) and Richie Benaud (6-70 in 1955).
- The stand of 202 by Glenn Maxwell and Cummins wasn't the highest ODI partnership in history, but it was the first time an eighth-wicket partnership passed 200 runs.

THE CAPTAIN'S YEAR

FORMAT	MATCHES	WON	LOST	DRAWN
Test	11	7	2	2
ODI	24	15	9	0
Total	33	25	6	2

*Cummins didn't play in the final two Tests against India or the ODI series in South Africa. Includes ICC trophy matches.

BOWLING

FORMAT	INNINGS	WICKETS	AVERAGE	ECONOMY RATE
Test	19	42	27.5	3.6
ODI	13	17	36.3	5.7

*excludes 10 World Cup matches

In terms of Test matches, a downside for Cummins was that the unhappy series in India ended his reign as No.1 ranked bowler in Test cricket. He'd been top since 2019.

He lost the ranking to James Anderson, the Englishman taking top place for the sixth time in his career, at the Age of 40 this time.

Anderson played his first Test in May 2003 v Zimbabwe at Lord's. He was part of three victorious Ashes campaigns against Australia and announced his retirement on 11 May 2024.

Australia had a relatively light schedule at the start of 2024. The year began with a trip across "the ditch" for Cummins and his team.

Clashes between the neighbours are always keenly contested.

February 2024 was no exception, and it wasn't surprising that the captain was the one who stepped up with bat and ball to secure a three-wicket win in Christchurch. He took four second-innings wickets then posted 32 not out in an unbeaten partnership with Alex Cary (64 not out) to chase down the 279 runs needed for victory and seal the series 2-0 after winning the first Test by 172 runs.

What would be the skipper's lingering memories of the stellar 2023 year?

"You've got to go and win a World Cup," Cummins said. "You just can't wait for it to happen.

"With our batting particularly, you saw the openers going out really aggressive and pretty much didn't waver from that for the rest of the tournament.

"I think we saved our best for last. And a couple of big-match players stood up and, yeah, we're pretty chuffed.

"You can't go past the World Cup final. I think that's going to be that one moment that once it's all done, the career's finished, I'm going to look back on it as a career highlight."

2

FROM ASHES TO ASHES

The managements of the Australian and English teams went through an upheaval between the 2021-22 Ashes series in Australia and the return series in England in 2023.

There was one constant when the dust settled, however; Australia still had The Urn.

Australia went into the home Ashes series with Pat Cummins as the new captain, appointed on 26 November 2021 and leading his team out for the first Ashes test on 8 December. Justin Langer was coach.

By the time the Australians arrived in England mid-2023 for the return series, Langer had gone, replaced by Andrew McDonald, and Cummins had led Australia to a 4-0 Ashes triumph on home turf.

England's process followed a different path. Those in charge of English cricket were not at all amused by the team's performance in Australia, failing to win a Test with a draw the best result in five attempts. Joe Root stood down as captain in 2022.

After the squad returned home, coach Chris Silverwood and director of cricket Ashley Giles moved on, gone in February. England won 10 of 29 Tests under Silverwood.

Former player (by now Sir) Andrew Strauss temporarily took over from Giles and appointed former player Paul Collingwood as interim coach for the tour of the West Indies in March.

The three-Tests tour of West Indies didn't go well, England losing 1-0 with two draws.

Back home, Collingwood was replaced by 40-year-old former

New Zealand captain Brendon McCullum, in May 2022. To that point England had only won one Test of its previous 17.

McCullum said he aimed to "move the team forward into a more successful era" with new captain Ben Stokes, who had replaced Joe Root in April.

"In taking this role on, I am acutely aware of the significant challenges the team faces at present, and I strongly believe in my ability to help the team emerge as a stronger force once we've confronted them head-on," McCullum said.

The improvement in fortunes was immediate. England won 10 of its next 11 Test matches, with one loss.

McCullum's first assignment was a two-Test series at home against his old team, New Zealand. England won the first Test comfortably but lost the second by one run. Not the ideal start.

In contrast to England after the drubbing it copped from Australia in 2021-22, Pat Cummins' team looked to be settled. Cummins was roundly hailed for holding the Ashes and not conceding a Test to the visitors. He was everybody's hero.

But rumblings surfaced soon after the Ashes series ended in 2022 about the future of coach Justin Langer, despite his record. By the end of February Langer was gone, not happily, and replaced by the 41-year-old McDonald.

McCullum and McDonald were chalk-and-cheese as far as their records were concerned.

McDonald was probably considered a bowling all-rounder in his early playing days.

In 2006-07, McDonald became only the fifth player in State-based competitions to make 750 runs and take 25 wickets in a season.

He played his first Test against South Africa in Sydney in 2009 before travelling to South Africa with the squad for the reverse series a few weeks later. He managed nine Test wickets at an average of 33.33. He scored 107 Test runs at an average of 21.4.

McDonald also played ODI cricket for Australia and more than 90

T20 matches, including stints in the Indian Premier League.

His first coaching gig after retiring as a player in 2016 was at Leicestershire in English county cricket. Then he oversaw the Melbourne Renegades in the Australian Big Bash League. Victoria won the Sheffield Shield national competition in his first year in charge there.

He also coached the Rajasthan Royals in the IPL, 2018-19.

He was first appointed interim coach of the national side before permanency in April 2022.

McCullum played 101 Test matches for New Zealand, scoring 6,543 runs at an average of 38.64 before retiring from Test cricket in 2016, deciding to become something of a "gun for hire" in the short form of the game.

He played for several teams through his career from 1996: Otago, Canterbury, Glamorgan, Kolkata Knight Riders, NSW, Sussex, Kochi Tuskers Kerala, Brisbane Heat, Chennai Super Kings, Warwickshire, Gujarat Lions, Middlesex, Trinbago Knight Riders, Lahore Qalandars, Sunrisers Hyderabad, Royal Challengers Bangalore and Kandahar Kris.

He coached Kolkata Knight Riders in 2020-21.

He hadn't been in charge of England for long when his approach to the game became known as "Bazball".

The Australians under McDonald and Cummins were to see Bazball first-hand in 2023. But some of the Australians probably saw its beginnings in New Zealand several years earlier.

Cummins wasn't in the squad that faced New Zealand in Christchurch in the second Test in 2016.

The record shows Australia won the Test by seven wickets, thanks mainly to centuries by Joe Burns and Steve Smith in a first innings total of 505.

The record also shows New Zealand captain Brendon McCullum, batting in the middle order, blasted his way to 149 runs from 75 balls in what was then the fastest century in Test history.

The word "Bazball" hadn't been coined then. It was more simply just "Baz," the nickname of McCullum.

The Kiwi captain wasn't trying to revolutionise the game then – that would come later. Instead, he said, he was simply trying to belt every ball he faced to or beyond the boundary.

Cummins was around in time to see Baz in action for the Brisbane Heat in Australia's Big Bash T20 competition when the "Bash Brothers" took centre stage. McCullum and Chris Lynn became smash hits.

Their effect was no more obvious than in a game against the Hobart Hurricanes. The Heat were set a target of 175 runs. The Bash Brothers helped chase that down in just 8.5 overs, in a partnership of 109.

It seemed all-out attack was going to be McCullum's trademark wherever he went.

Cummins and the Australians would have known what to expect when they arrived in England in 2023 for the Ashes "re-match". The English players would be taking a different approach to that when they capitulated in Australia a few months earlier.

There was much hype about Bazball.

Cummins conceded the rejuvenated England Test side's achievements over the past 12 months leading up to the 2023 series had been "impressive".

But, he said, the Australians wouldn't be led into trying to replicate England's style of play.

The numbers spoke for themselves: McCullum's England side by then had won 10 of 12 Test matches and scored at 4.76 runs an over – more than a run an over better than any other Test side. The success included a 3-0 win over Pakistan on the sub-continent.

To sum up, England had looked capable of winning from any position, something that was beyond them as they were demolished in the 2021-22 series in Australia.

At the end of the series, Cummins was asked how the Australians had coped with Bazball.

It had appeared the English pitches were prepared to suit the attacking players.

"The pitches were actually quite different to what we'd previously experienced in England," Cummins said. "More like a one-day pitch. But while in one regard the game was also faster-paced, because of the way they were trying to bat, it always felt like you were close to getting wickets. So I didn't mind it, to be honest."

In terms of helping England win back The Urn, it would be difficult to say Bazball was a resounding success.

Australia held the Ashes after their 4-0 success in the series at home in 2017-18 and retained them in England in a 2-2 drawn series in 2019. Funny how history can repeat itself. That was the same outcome in 2021-22 and again in 2023.

The 2021-22 Ashes series was well documented in Ron Reed's book *Captain Pat*, in 2022.

Pat Cummins' report card from his first term in charge of the Test team would be a pretty simple, straightforward document. He got at least an A, probably an A-plus, as noted by Reed: "He led the team in four of the five Ashes matches and won three of them by big margins. He fell just one wicket short of doing the same in the other one and despite missing one match through no fault of his own he took more wickets than any other bowler on either side."

It was the third successive time in an Ashes series that Cummins had been leading wicket-taker. Even after missing the second Test due to Covid protocols, he had 21 wickets in four matches.

FROM ASHES TO ASHES

The 2021-22 series summary:
- It was Australia's 34th series win against England. England had won 32 of 72 Ashes series. Six were drawn.
- England's batting average was 19.18, the lowest for any team in a five-match Test series since 2001. It was also England's worst batting average in an Ashes series since 1890, when they averaged 15.74 over the two matches.
- Six times in 10 innings England failed to pass 200 and not once managed 300.
- Only one wicket in Sydney stood between England and the ignominy of a third 5-0 series whitewash in 15 years.
- Australia had won all 10 day-night Tests they had played, three of them against England, including two in the 2021-22 Ashes series. Australian batsmen averaged 33.87 and the bowlers averaged 20.83 in those 10 Tests.
- The Hobart result marked 15 consecutive Tests for England in Australia without a win, sharing the second-longest streak without a Test win for any team in Australia. New Zealand played 18 Tests between their victories in 1985 and 2011. Sri Lanka played 15 Tests in Australia without a win.
- Joe Root as skipper had lost 10 Tests. Only Archie McLaren with 11 had lost more. Eight of Root's 10 losses were in Australia.
- Scott Boland's bowling average in the Ashes series was 9.55. Only two players with 15-plus wickets in their debut Test series had a better bowling average than Boland; 8.50 by Narendra Hirwani and 9.47 by Charlie Turner.
- Player of the series was Travis Head (Compton-Miller Medal).
- Joe Root stepped down as England Captain in April 2022, saying the job had taken a heavy toll on him after dispiriting tours of Australia and the Caribbean and a string of poor results. Two years later he questioned whether England should have bothered to undertake the tour amid Australia's stringent Covid protocols.

The English went home to lick their wounds, hoping for a re-build before Australia turned up for a five-Test series on English turf in mid-2023 where they would be confronted by Bazball.

• • •

Pat Cummins may have had a lot on his mind when it came to the return Ashes series in 2023.

His team had just a week earlier celebrated winning the World Test Championship against India in London. Also, he'd been made captain of Australia's one-day team for the looming World Cup in ODI cricket in India.

But the Ashes in England was the immediate priority. Even a drawn series would be good enough for Australia to get done the job of retaining the Ashes.

Would Bazball be a factor?

The series turned out to be one of the most fiercely contested of the modern era, and not without controversy.

Australia didn't seem fazed by the much-vaunted Bazball-playing England and retained The Ashes after five dramatic contests.

A feature of the series was that neither team was dismissed for less than 220 runs. Four matches were decided by fewer than 50 runs or by three or fewer wickets.

The first two Tests went Australia's way. But the Australians found themselves under pressure in the third Test at Headingly. Worse, they'd lost Nathan Lyon. The record-making off-spinner had gone home after suffering a series-ending calf injury while fielding in the deep in the second Test.

Lyon believed he would have helped Australia win the Ashes instead of managing a draw. "I do believe if I was here it would have been 4-0 to Australia," he said in a BBC interview while playing county cricket in England in 2024. (Just for the record, Lyon made his Test debut in 2011, played 123 test matches to 2024 for Australia delivering 31,614 balls and claiming 501 wickets yet did not once bowl a front-foot no-ball.

And he might be around for a few more years yet). When it came to who was Australia's' greatest off-spinner, Lyon was the Greatest Of All Time (GOAT).

Bazball was evident in the fourth Test at Old Trafford, England looking for all the world like a one-day side or even a T20 side as the batters went on the attack. England made 592 in reply to Australia's 317. Opener Zac Crawley topped the list with 189 runs from 182 balls.

A win in the fourth Test at Old Trafford would have levelled the series with the final Test to be the decider. After England's first innings the odds were clearly against the visitors.

But an England victory wasn't to be.

The intervention of rain at Old Trafford cost England any chance of snatching back The Urn. Australia was in deep strife at five wickets down and still trailing by 61 runs when a halt to play was called. A draw was a good outcome for the visitors, a get-out-of-jail result.

England went on to win the final Test, but a 2-2 series draw was good enough for Australia to retain the Ashes.

Although the drawn Test saved the Aussies in the series, there was plenty of chatter, social media carrying most of it.

Incredibly, the Old Trafford result left some pundits speculating on Cummin's future. How quickly a few pundits could turn on him!

Five dropped catches by fielders had proved costly and, as well, Cummins copped plenty of stick for his tactics.

He was accused of being timid, too defensive and lacking direction in the field.

Former Australian Test captain Ian Chappell branded some of Pat Cummins' tactics in Manchester as "stupidity".

He criticised the decision to protect the boundary early in the innings of England's top-order batters, seemingly happy to give up plenty of singles but allowing the batters to ease into their innings.

Former Australian great fast bowler Glen McGrath was another critic: "Pat Cummins just looks a little bit tired and jaded to me, and that was always a risk of having a fast bowler as captain. It's one of those things; it's about momentum, it's about energy. England's got the momentum now, and it's always hard to steal it back off the team that has it, especially when they're playing well."

Another of the criticisms was that Cummins himself didn't open the bowling.

Former Victoria wicketkeeper Darren Berry suggested on social media that Cummins would quit at the end of the series. As usual with most social media sports commentary, those making the noise had the word "former" before their names.

Berry posted: "Pat Cummins is a magnificent cricketer no doubt but remember this msg. He will resign from the captaincy after the Ashes series."

After the later home series against Pakistan, Berry was happy to recant, posting on X: "Pat Cummins I was wrong. I questioned your tactical nous and your tenure as skipper during the frustrating Ashes series. Once again today at the G you have led our country over the line with your big (heart emoji) & immense skill, they were never in question. I'm so happy to eat my words."

Anyway, Cummins and McDonald quickly laid to rest any nonsense about Cummins' future. Absolutely nothing doing on that front. And the views of all the "formers" were consigned to an appropriate place.

Cummins and coach McDonald did acknowledge there were plenty of reasonable criticisms to be made of the tactical and playing performance at Old Trafford. It was, after all, Australia's worst match of the tour.

Astute watchers of cricket noticed something out of character happening on the field.

One observer who picked up on something not typical of Australian teams was former England captain-cum-commentator, Nasser Hussein.

"Often when you look down at an Australian side historically, you know who the captain is, whether it be Taylor, Border, Ponting, Waugh," Hussein said.

FROM ASHES TO ASHES

"You look down today and there's been a lot of cricketers waving their arms around."

Was there anything to it?

According to the 24 May 2024 instalment of the Amazon Prime Video series "The Test" there was some tension within the Australian camp.

The documentary revealed these exchanges:

Cummins: "Marnus (Labuschagne) always has ideas, Smithy's always waving his arms around at first slip."

Smith: "I offer advice all the time. It's just whether we want to use it and that's up to the captain to make that decision ultimately."

Labuschagne: "Creatively I think we could have just tried more things…tried different stuff for different times and if it didn't work, I don't think we were worse off than we would've been…changing it up, setting a really obscure field or doing something really different. It's hard, I can give you my own views of what I would've done, but…enough said."

And just as you would expect from a top-class leader, the captain brushed all the noise aside after the match to get on with the job in the final Test of the series, at The Oval.

His decision to bowl first on a juicy wicket looked like a masterstroke.

On a personal level, he produced probably his best bowling of the series with his first spell of the day, beating the batters often and smashing the ball into Zak Crawley several times before dismissing him for 22.

Australia seemed on track to win the Ashes outright (leading the series 2-1 at the time) and claim a first series victory in England since 2001. But that wasn't to be either.

A batting collapse when Australia lost five wickets in half an hour saw England take victory by 49 runs and level the series at 2-2 (one match drawn).

The English press seemed to think their team was the better in the series, one scribe saying the fearless Bazball approach had seen England emerge as "perhaps the most entertaining Test team in history".

A big statement and one England might struggle to live up to.

Summing up the series, that same scribe had one last swipe at Australia over the runout of Johnny Bairstow in the second Test, at Lord's.

"Australia's most lasting highlight, by contrast, was Alex Carey's stumping of Jonny Bairstow, an act of such dastardly opportunism that protocols in the Long Room might never be the same again," the writer said.

The Bairstow incident after much debate and some ugly scenes in the Long Room boiled down to the straightforward question of whether he should have been stumped by Carey when he left his crease after the last ball of an over, but "over" hadn't been called. The rules were clear but was the action in the "spirit of the game?"

Cummins copped criticism from many in England – and a few in Australia – for not recalling Bairstow to the crease after he was given out. More on that later.

Journalist Andrew Clark (Channel Nine Newspapers) summed up the Ashes in England: "The 2023 series was marked by fast-paced centuries by English captain Ben Stokes and opener Zak Crawley, fine batting by Australian opener Usman Khawaja, brilliant bowling by Australian captain Pat Cummins and fellow speedster Mitchell Starc, and an all-round outstanding display by English quick and late-order batter Chris Woakes."

It's worth noting that Usman Khawaja batted for more balls (a total of 1,263) than any player in a series since 2002 (Rahul Dravid, India) and more than any Australian in England since David Boon in 1993.

Clark opined that the 2023 series "generated more interest in almost 150 years of Ashes Test cricket than any other series, apart from the 1948 Australian Invincibles tour of England and the controversial 1932-33 Bodyline Tests in Australia."

FROM ASHES TO ASHES

How the series unfolded:

First Test (Edgbaston): Pat Cummins saved Australia, not with the ball but with the bat, guiding his side to a thrilling victory. Australia needed 51 runs in the last hour with Cummins and Nathan Lyon batting. A seemingly spectacular catch by Stuart Broad looked to have sent Lyon on his way. But upon review it was found not to be a fair catch, and Cummins and Lyon saw Australia safely over the line. Usman Khawaja was player of the match with innings of 141 and 65 as Australia won by two wickets with 27 balls remaining. Cummins contributed to Australia's win with 44 not out in the second innings. He took 4-63 in England's second innings. Joe Root made 118 not out in England's first innings, Nathan Lyon took 4-149 from 29 overs in England's first innings.

Second Test (Lord's): England won the toss and sent Australia in. Australia took a 2-0 lead with Steve Smith's innings of 110 and 34 getting the player of the match award. Travis Head scored 77 runs in Australia's first innings and claimed 2-17 in England's first innings. Khawaja made 77 in Australia's second innings. Cummins took 3-69 in England's second innings in which new captain Ben Stokes made 155. Australia won by 43 runs.

Third Test (Headingly): England won by three-wickets after Australia had a first innings lead. English pacemen Mark Wood (player of the match) and Chris Woakes took eight first innings wickets between them, a feat matched by Cummins (6-91) and Starc in England's first innings. Mitchell Marsh made 118 in Australia's first innings. Broad and Woakes each took three wickets in Australia's second innings, Head made 77 and Marsh 43. Brook's 73 helped England to victory.

Fourth Test (Old Trafford): Australia escaped with a draw thanks to the weather. After making only a just-passable first innings total of 317 (Marsh and Labuschagne both 51) after being sent in, Australia struggled to restrain England which replied with 592 (player of the match Crawley made 189 and Bairstow 99 not out). The Australians were 5-214 in reply when rain intervened. It was unlikely the remaining batters could have posted a sufficient score to cause England any grief, even if they had managed to force the home side to bat again. Labuschagne scored 111 in the second innings.

Fifth Test (The Oval): With the Ashes on the line, Cummins won the toss and decided to bowl. England made a modest total of 283 (Brook 85). Starc took 4-82 and new Test spinner Todd Murphy (in for Lyon) 2-22. Australia took a first innings lead of just 12 runs (Smith 71, Khawaja 47). Woakes was player of the match taking 3-6 and 4-50 And making 36 runs. England made a much better fist of the second innings with 395 (Root 91). Starc took 4-100 and Murphy 4-110. Australia needed an imposing 384 for victory, an unlikely total in terms of Test match history. But thanks to Khawaja (72) and David Warner (60) the Australians got close.

This match wasn't without controversy either. With Australia perhaps on track for their first Ashes series victory in the UK since Steve Waugh's team in 2001 and chasing down the target of 384, a ball change was made.

Opener Usman Khawaja was hit on the helmet by England fast bowler Mark Wood and England complained to the umpires that the ball had lost its shape in the incident. The umpires chose a seemingly newer ball from a box of 12 used ones. The different ball had an immediate effect, seaming more than the previous one and Australia crumbled to finish 49 runs short.

England's commitment to the spirit of cricket was questioned on day five when England players thought captain Ben Stokes had taken a catch to dismiss Steve Smith. The umpire said not out. It was apparent Stokes was worried that he hadn't controlled the catch when the ball slipped from his grasp as he raised his arms to appeal. He sought a review anyway, urged on by teammates. The review was unsuccessful under Law 33 ("The act of making a catch shall start from the time when the ball first comes into a contact with a fielder's person and shall end when a fielder obtains complete control over both the ball and their own movement").

Australian opener Usman Khawaja was easily the best-performed batter in the first three Tests and another good knock in the final Test saw him amass 496 to be the top run-scorer of the series.

Mitchell Starc found his form towards the end of the series and his 23 wickets was the best result of all the bowlers, shading retiring England paceman Stuart Broad by one. Cummins took 18 wickets for the series.

Before the Ashes series and after the World Test Championship Cummins was asked about how his era in charge would be defined, not that there was any sign that it was coming to an end.

He said lifting the Ashes urn aloft would be a legacy-definer.

"The great thing about this (championship) final is we feel like we've played awesome cricket for the last two years and being there at the end holding the trophy feels really well deserved. That's great for our team," said the proud skipper.

"But I'd say whether we like it or not, Ashes tend to define eras and teams. Ashes are bloody hard to win. I think it's been 20-odd years.

"It's not going to be easy – but if we were to win it, that is legacy-defining stuff." A drawn series would have to suffice.

That was not to underplay the significance of what Australia had achieved.

After the Ashes series, Cummins acknowledged that Australia "fell a little short of the goal" but was proud of his players for retaining the Ashes.

"Two-two seems fair, and it was a wonderful series," Cummins said. "It was two high-quality teams. It seemed like every session we shared the honours.

"From the start we said we were over here to win the Ashes. We can be hugely proud of retaining the Ashes – it's no easy feat against a high-quality England in their own conditions – but of course we wanted to come over here and win."

With the series drawn 2-2, Australia could rest easy with the Ashes safely within keeping at least until 2025-26.

• • •

The Ashes Urn is not used as the official trophy, but replicas are given to the winning side at the end of each Ashes series. The original urn remains in the Marylebone Cricket Club Museum in the Lord's ground, regardless of which country wins a series and is displayed with a scorecard from the 1882 match where the trophy originated.

On 29 August 1882 England were defeated by seven runs in one of the most famous collapses in cricketing history. It was Australia's first victory over the full strength of England in England.

The next day the *Sporting Times* published a mock "obituary" to English cricket.

While in Australia for a return series in November 1882, a small urn, thought to contain the ashes of a bail used in the third match, was presented to England captain Ivo Bligh by a group of women, among them Janet Lady Clarke and Florence Morphy. Lady Clarke's husband, Sir William Clarke, was president of the Melbourne Cricket Club and instrumental in having Bligh's team visit Australia. Florence Murphy later married Ivo Bligh.

FROM ASHES TO ASHES

The text on the urn reads:
"When Ivo goes back with the urn, the urn; Studds, Steel, Read and Tylecote return, return; The welkin will ring loud, The great crowd will feel proud, Seeing Barlow and Bates with the urn, the urn; And the rest coming home with the urn."

In 1998, Bligh's 82-year-old daughter-in-law said the urn actually contained the remains of her mother-in-law's veil. Some people also believe it holds the remains of a burnt ball cover.

The Urn is made of red terracotta and is about 10.5cm tall. It has made two visits to Australia, in 1988 and 2006.

POSTSCRIPT: The word "Bazball" found its way into the Collins English Dictionary in 2023. The entry: "NOUN. A style of Test cricket in which the batting side attempts to gain the initiative by playing in a highly aggressive manner. Word origin:…after Brendon McCullum, known as Baz (born 1981), New Zealand cricketer and coach."

The Australians were a little non-plussed. Marnus Labuschagne described the inclusion of Bazball in the dictionary as "garbage". "Seriously I don't know what that is, honestly," he said. Steve Smith also laughed when asked about it when in India for the World Cup. "Guys just keep joking about it," he said. "I think Ronnie (Australian coach Andrew McDonald) has had enough of hearing about Bazball to be honest."

Australian off-spinner Nathan Lyon wasn't too worried about what England's style was called.

"I don't mind hearing about it. It's their type of cricket. I just feel like we've been playing entertaining cricket for a number of years now, we just don't need to call it a name to justify it," he said in a BBC interview.

"I've seen David Warner score centuries in a session well and truly before Bazball was invented.

"It's up to them to keep doing it now. They've literally got to go at six runs an over otherwise they're not playing Bazball. If you're going to talk about it, you've got to do it."

Even England eventually seemed to reject Bazball as a suitable term for the cricket that McCullum had his team playing.

As for the man himself, McCullum thought it "silly" when it was coined in 2022. "There's actually quite a bit of thought that goes into how the guys manufacture their performances and when they put pressure on bowlers and which bowlers they put pressure on," he told Australian radio station SEN. "There's also times when they've absorbed pressure beautifully as well."

One Australian who was impressed by Bazball was Tottenham Hotspur football manager Ange Postecoglou, whose attacking style with Spurs in the English Premier League became known as "Angeball."

Postecoglou was at Lord's watching the Australia-England Test match in 2023 just before taking up the Spurs appointment.

He told Sky Sports: "I love Bazball mate, I think it's brilliant," he said.

"In any sport, when I see teams kind of break the traditional mould, that's when people get really uneasy about it – and that's when you know, 'OK, this could be something special'.

"It's not guaranteed to work. It could all fall to pieces and end up in tears. But when you make people uneasy and uncomfortable with what they see it probably means you're breaking new ground and I love that in anything in life.

"That's where the special stuff exists and that's the kind of space I'm in."

Postecoglou's attacking football lifted Spurs from 8th in the EPL the previous season to fifth in 2024, and into European football.

FOOTNOTE: The Ashes between England and Australia is not the oldest cricket rivalry in the world. Before the Ashes came about, America and Canada played the world's first international cricket match in 1844. Canada won by 23 runs in the three-day match on Staten Island, New York.

3
A TEST OF THE BEST

World Test Championship final June 2023, The Oval, London. Australia v India

MATCH SUMMARY

Australia: First innings: 469 all out (Head 163, Smith 121).
India: First innings: 296 all out (Rahane 89; Cummins 3-83, Green 2-44).
Australia second innings: 8-270 declared (Carey 46, Labuschagne 41).
India second innings: 234 all out (Kohli 49, Rahane 48; Lyon 4-41, Boland 3-46).

Australia wins by 209 runs

The man who described his batting technique as "not the prettiest thing in the world" provided Australia with the springboard to collect the World Test Championship at The Oval in South London on 7 June 2023.

When Travis Head went to the wicket, he could have imagined he was in India. Australia was playing India in the final and there was no doubt about which team most fans were supporting. Blue and orange was the most popular colour combo in the stands. To be fair, green and yellow was evident.

At that point on day one, just after lunch, Australia had lost 3-76 on a greenish wicket after being sent in. India left out off-spinner Ravi Ashwin, a decision the team might have rued later.

Australia had a task ahead of them to see off some good new-ball bowling by Mohammed Shami and Mohammed Siraj.

India was without Jasprit Bumrah whose pace was most impressive on his visits to Australia in 2018-19 and 2020-21. He was recovering from recent back surgery in New Zealand.

India would love to have had Bumrah operating when Travis Head went to the pitch. A brilliant Bumrah yorker dispatched Head in the 2018 Boxing Day Test in Melbourne. He got him again in the 2020-21 series, again with a lethal delivery.

There was no Bumrah this time.

India seemed to have the wood on Australia in recent Tests, winning the series 2-1 in 2018-19; 2-1 in 2020-21, both in Australia; then 2-1 at home in 2022-23.

Australia would need something special in the WTC final to reverse the worrying history that was developing.

The innings by Head and the Australians' bowling performance on the fifth day was special.

Head didn't waste time getting down to work at The Oval. He faced four balls before lashing out with back-to-back boundaries, from the fifth and sixth balls. He scored at a brisk pace thereafter.

He made 163 from 174 balls, ably supported by Steve Smith who made 121 to set Australia up with an impressive total of 469.

In reply, India made 296, Cummins taking 3-83 from 20 overs.

Australia's second innings wasn't as steady as the first, but a declaration at 8-270 gave India a seemingly impossible target for victory. Head made only 18 this time; Carey was best, not out 66.

Chasing 444, the Indians were all out for 234 before lunch on day five (Sunday) after losing seven wickets on the final morning. Australia won by 209 runs.

Cummins managed only one wicket in India's run chase as the pitch seemed more receptive to spin than it had been earlier. Nathan Lyon took four wickets.

Boland, hero of the Ashes Boxing Test back in Melbourne in 2021, took three for a match-total of five. Despite his efforts Boland was always going to be the odd man out when Cummins, Hazlewood and Starc were all fit and firing. Boland was 32 when he made his debut in the 2021-2022 Ashes series.

Boland and Steve Smith provided what was probably the turning point of the WTC game.

India began the final day needing 280 with seven wickets in hand. The fourth-wicket stand between Virat Kohli and Ajinkya Rahane had been worth 71 and the pair had looked comfortable.

Australia wasted a review when India was 3-179, wrongly thinking it might have had Kohli's wicket.

But just two balls later the Australians had the breakthrough.

Boland's line and length kept the scoring under control until the sucker-ball he served up to Kohli in the seventh over of the day. It was wider and fuller than he had been pitching them to that point.

The Indian champion saw a chance to put the Boland delivery away with a trademark drive, but managed only to get an edge that flew towards the vacant third-slip space. Smith leapt to his right and with both feet off the ground grasped the ball. Indian hopes dived in that moment too, Kohli out for 49.

Two balls later, Boland had all-rounder Ravindra Jadeja out for a duck, edging a ball to keeper Carey.

"It was a big partnership to break, his (Boland's) spell was outstanding," Smith said.

"He bowled beautifully, got a couple of key breakthroughs, and got us on our way.

"It was a great lead-in from Baz (Boland), it was a really good spell, beat the bat a few times and looked threatening."

Boland's key wickets helped see India collapse on the morning of the last day, losing 7-55 from 23.3 overs, the match ending just on the scheduled lunch break.

Boland finished the match with 5-105 including 3-46 in India's second innings.

It must be remembered that his Boxing Day Test rout of England in 2021 gave Australia the perfect start to their WTC campaign. Boland almost single-handedly demolished England in one of the most spectacular Test debuts of all time when he grabbed four wickets in 19 balls to finish with the amazing figures of 6-7 from four overs in England's second innings.

That Boxing Day Test victory by an innings and 14 runs earned maximum points for Australia's World Test Championship ranking that eventually saw Cummins' men on the way to England for the final.

After the win at The Oval, Cummins heaped praise on his men for their effort.

"That's one of the most satisfying bits," he said. "Obviously the win here, but to make it to the final you've got to win everywhere in the world.

"I think this cycle was 20 Test matches and I think we might have only lost three or four.

"The boys were fantastic the whole way through, we adapted well and that's what makes this so satisfying."

Would Boland have played if Josh Hazelwood hadn't been ruled out with a side and Achilles injury? Maybe not, but he remained in the team for the Ashes Test at Leeds in July, his last Test appearance for the year.

In 2024, Boland played English Country cricket until injury forced him out, three Sheffield Shield matches for Victoria (19 wickets) and a T20 game for the Melbourne Stars in the Big Bash.

The World Test championship came with monetary rewards. Australia received a cash prize of $US 1.6 million and India received $US 800,000.

The win meant Australia had become the first team to hold trophies of all ICC tournaments across the three cricket formats, though not all at the same time.

And, of course, it was yet another deserved feather in the cap of skipper Pat Cummins.

A TEST OF THE BEST

Leading WTC run-scorers: Travis Head (AUS) 181; Steven Smith (AUS) 155; Ajinkya Rahane (IND) 135; Alex Carey (AUS) 114; Marnus Labuschagne (AUS) 67.

Most wickets: Scott Boland (AUS) 5; Nathan Lyon (AUS) 5; Mohammed Siraj (IND) 5; Ravindra Jadeja (IND) 4; Mohammad Shami (IND) 4.

Man of the Match: Travis Head.

Head did face Bumrah a few months later, in the ODI World Cup in India, and seemed to have the paceman's measure. He made 137 (Siraj claiming his wicket); Bumrah took 2-43.

The Ashes Test series in England that followed the WTC match in 2023 marked the end of David Warner's overseas Test and ODI careers. He played his last matches for Australia at home during the Pakistan tour; his last Test was against Pakistan in Sydney in 2024.

Warner continued to play in the T20 format but was omitted by the Delhi Capitals in 2024 due to poor form and injury (37 runs in four innings) and replaced by another Australian, Jake Fraser McGurk. Former Australian captain Ricky Ponting was coach of the team but his contract was not renewed for 2025.

In possibly his last campaign for an Australian team, Warner headed off to the US and the Caribbean for the World T20I Cup. He managed some good scores in the preliminary rounds but managed only a total of 11 runs in the last two Super 8s games; not the way he would have hoped to end his career for Australia.

Cummins finished 2023-24 with 42 Test wickets, second only to teammate Nathan Lyon and rounding off the season with a 10-wicket haul against Pakistan, the second of his career.

The World Test championship is played over a two-year cycle. The 2023 final marked the end of the second edition.

Australia qualified for the final by winning the third Test of the 2022–23 Border-Gavaskar Trophy in India. India qualified after Sri Lanka failed to win the first match of their series in New Zealand.

Points are accrued through the series that involve the 12 Test-playing nations: Australia, India, England, Pakistan, West Indies, South Africa, Sril Lanka, New Zealand, Zimbabwe, Bangladesh, Ireland and Afghanistan.

Scheduling remains a challenge as the world cricket program is cluttered, thanks mainly to the proliferation of short-form events, including India's IPL T20 tournament that remains firmly in the control of the BCCI (Indian's cricket ruling body).

To the end of 2023, Australia had won 10 ICC trophies across all formats of international cricket since championship trophies were introduced in 1975, contested over multi-year cycles. Titles included the ICC Cricket World Cup, ICC Champions Trophy, ICC T20 World Cup and the ICC World Test Championship.

The WTC first series began in 2019 and was won by New Zealand when a reserve day was used to compensate for a day's play lost to rain. The 2023 decider at The Oval was the end of the second edition.

Pat Cummins: "It's been an amazing two years. We've had this final in the diary for a while. It's been something we've been building up for so it's something we're going to savour.

"I know we've got a big series coming up, but we can worry about that in a couple days' time. You only get a few of these moments in your career where you can sit back, acknowledge a pretty special achievement – and that's one of these times."

Proponents of the Test championship were former West Indies captain Clive Lloyd and New Zealander Martin Crowe. The WTC replaced the ICC Champions Trophy last held in 2013.

The series has been scheduled for at least two more cycles, with finals set for 2025 and 2027. The 2023-25 cycle began with the 1st Ashes Test in June 2023.

As of May 2024, Australia led the Test team rankings with 3,715 points for a ranking of 124, ahead of India with a ranking of 120. Next came England and South Africa.

The WTC points system: 12 points for a win; 4 points for each team in a draw; 6 points for each team for a tie. A penalty is involved for slow over-rates – teams are docked a point for each over they fall behind.

As well as points towards the World Test championship most Test series have an individual trophy on the line.

England and Australia compete for The Ashes (since 1882-83 and the oldest); England and India play for the Anthony de Mello Trophy (and previously the Pataudi Trophy), the West Indies and Australia play for the Sir Frank Worrell Trophy; The West Indies and England play for the Wisden Trophy; Australian and New Zealand play for the Trans-Tasman Trophy; Australia and India play for the Border-Gavaskar Trophy; Australia and Zimbabwe play for the Southern Cross Trophy; West Indies and Zimbabwe play for the Clive Lloyd Trophy; India and South Africa play for the Freedom Trophy; the West Indies and Sri Lanka play for the Sobers-Tissera Trophy; Pakistan and Australia play for the Benaud-Qadar Trophy, and England and the West Indies play for the Richards-Botham Trophy.

Australia is the only team to have won more than 400 Test matches (408 by mid-2024). Second is England with just more than 380. Australia had lost 231 Tests and drawn 217, with a winning percentage of 47.49, the highest of Test-playing teams.

The two teams have also played more matches compared to other teams. England has played more than 1,000 red-ball (including pink-ball) games overall, the only team to do so.

AUSTRALIA'S PATH TO WORLD TEST CHAMPIONSHIP GLORY

Nov-Dec 2021-22
Australia beat England by nine wickets in Brisbane
Australia beat England by 275 runs in Adelaide
Australia beat England by an inns & 146 runs in Melbourne
Australia drew with England in Sydney
Australia beat England by 146 runs in Hobart

March 2022
Australia drew with Pakistan in Rawalpindi
Australia drew with Pakistan in Karachi
Australia beat Pakistan by 115 runs in Lahore

June 2022
Australia beat Sri Lanka by 10 wickets in Galle
Australia lost to Sri Lanka by an inns & 139 runs in Galle

Nov-Dec 2022
Australia beat West Indies by 164 runs in Perth
Australia beat West Indies by 419 runs in Adelaide

Dec-Jan 2022-23
Australia beat South Africa by six wickets in Brisbane
Australia beat South Africa by an inns & 182 runs in Melbourne
Australia drew with South Africa in Sydney

Feb-Mar 2023
Australia lost to India by an inns & 132 runs in Nagpur
Australia lost to India by six wickets in Delhi
Australia beat India by nine wickets in Indore
Australia drew with India in Ahmedabad

A TEST OF THE BEST

June 2023 (Championship final)
Australia beat India by 209 runs at The Oval, England.

Leading run-scorers
Usman Khawaja: 1,621 runs at an average of 64.84
Marnus Labuschagne: 1,576 runs at 52.53
Steve Smith: 1,407 runs at 52.11
Travis Head: 1,389 runs at 55.56

Leading wicket-takers
Nathan Lyon: 88 wickets at 26.12
Pat Cummins: 57 wickets at 22.15
Mitchell Starc: 55 wickets at 27.98
Scott Boland: 33 wickets at 14.57

Players used: Ashton Agar, Scott Boland, Alex Carey, Pat Cummins, Cameron Green, Peter Handscomb, Marcus Harris, Josh Hazlewood, Travis Head, Usman Khawaja, Matt Kuhnemann, Marnus Labuschagne, Nathan Lyon, Todd Murphy, Michael Neser, Matt Renshaw, Jhye Richardson, Steve Smith, Mitchell Starc, Mitchell Swepson, David Warner.

4

ONE-DAY, SOME DAY!

Australia always finds a way and this has to go down as one of the great World Cup wins – for anyone, given the context of the tournament. India were undefeated and playing the best cricket. All their players were in form, 120,000 fans were expecting India to win, so this was some performance. It was a brave decision from Cummins to bowl first. A weak captain makes a decision that if it goes wrong and you lose it makes you look less bad. But he made a brave and right decision. He absolutely nailed it. He nailed everything. Field placements, bowling changes. Everything was spot on.

NASSER HUSSEIN, SKY SPORTS COMMENTATOR AND FORMER ENGLAND CAPTAIN

Pat Cummins sent India into bat in the final of the ODI World Cup at Ahmedabad on 19 November 2023!

WTF, the text messages would have screamed!

The underdog inviting the dominant team in the ODI World Cup preliminary rounds – undefeated, in fact – to bat first? On their home turf?

Surely it was suicide to invite the Indians to have first crack at the Australian bowling attack at home in such a big match.

That couldn't be right.

ONE-DAY, SOME DAY!

If there are such people as bookmakers in India, they would have installed the home-side as long odds-on favourites, even well before the combatants in the final were known. The odds would have been tweaked sharply when captain Cummins announced that he'd bowl. Bets might even have been rejected, so short would have been the price on the home team.

It isn't clear when the Australians decided they would field first.

"The crowd's obviously going to be very one-sided but, in sport, there's nothing more satisfying than hearing a big crowd go silent and that's the aim for us tomorrow," Cummins said on the eve of the game. Maybe he'd already decided, although he suggested later the decision was made on the day.

Australia won the World Cup, and according to Cummins, his team's home-crowd-silencing heroics on that day was the highlight of the year, maybe even his career.

"Last year (2023) was a wonderful year," Cummins told an interviewer in India in 2024. "Everything seemed to go right on the cricket field. But I think I can't go past the ODI World Cup. It only happens once every four years. To play in a World Cup is amazing, to reach a final in India in front of a huge Ahmedabad stadium, I don't think we'll ever beat that moment. That's a career highlight for me."

Cummins had led Australia only four times in ODIs before the 2023 World Cup. He also missed the ODI series against India after of the Border-Gavaskar Trophy in March 2023 when his mother died.

Any doubt about whether Cummins had broken the mould of what Australian captains should be, the decision to ask India to bat first at a packed-out Narendra Modi Stadium in Ahmedabad was put to rest, surely; a decision that set Cummins apart from all those who had gone before.

Confidence was high. The Australians entered the World Cup having won a Test in India (though losing the series 2-1), retained the Ashes in England and won the World Test Championship against India.

Were they over-confident? Doubtful, as their losses early in the tournament to India and South Africa would have given them – and those make-believe bookmakers – cause for thought.

Sending India in with the ICC World Cup trophy at stake raised more than just a few eyebrows. India had won all 10 of their lead-up games and were clear favourites.

Indian fans fell silent when Cummins called the toss correctly but roared with delight when he opted to field.

Former Test captain Alan Border in Melbourne's *Herald Sun* newspaper: "Pat Cummins' bowl-first call in the World Cup final was one of the bravest decisions I have seen from a cricket captain. I must be honest, when I heard Pat say 'we will bowl' I thought oh no, Patrick, you have lost the plot, you blokes! When Rohit Sharma was going hard early, I thought what are we doing?"

Former Aussie keeper Brad Haddin said on *Fox Cricket's* coverage: "I thought the Australians would have batted first, put runs on the board in the final and then let the final play out from there and Rohit Sharma has obviously read the conditions a lot different to what we did. You get first use of the surface we're not quite sure how it is going to play but I thought Australia would've batted first."

Prakash Wakankar of the BBC's *Test Match Special* had said after the toss: "I'm not an expert but are Australia overthinking the spin and the dew, hoping that it gets easier to bat second? But I am still surprised. I thought it was a certainty that whoever would win the toss would bat."

Not all commentators were as bemused. Former Test batsman Mark Waugh: "I guess there were maybe two reasons.

"The first reason is they're not sure how the pitch is going to play and often if that's the case you bowl first and the dew factor – that's a big part of the game if it does start to dew-up at night – then that's going to help the Australians."

Former Test spinner Kerry O'Keeffe said he was not surprised by the Cummins call because recent history at Ahmedabad had suggested the venue was "not so bad for chasing."

ONE-DAY, SOME DAY!

Cummins said after the match: "We were tossing it (batting second) up.

"We've been batting first for most of the tournament, but we thought tonight was a good chase night because it felt it might be a little bit easier and everyone was pretty keen to get out there.

"We were kind of umming and aahing right up until the toss really, but I thought (there was) half a chance of the wicket getting better tonight.

"In a World Cup game you can make a mistake bowling and it doesn't really matter too much, but if you make a mistake batting and you're under pressure it can be fatal.

"So I just felt like it was the right time to go out and have a bowl.

"We made it really clear in the group we're all-in on making sure we weren't the team that stood off today, we wanted to take the game on and play the way that got us to the final.

"Maybe that comes from playing other finals before, also maybe missing out on some other finals in different tournaments but the group today was as confident going to final as I've seen the team."

Indian skipper Rohit Sharma was to say later he would have opted to bat anyway.

As Sharma and Shubman Gill walked out into the cauldron before a sea of blue in the stands to open proceedings, you could sense most of the crowd of 100,000 – mostly Indian of course – felt it already was game over. Next in would be Indian hero and batting superstar Virat Kohli, the highest run-scorer in the tournament.

And hadn't India cleaned up Australia comfortably early in October in the first round of the tournament (Australia all out for 199 in 49.3 overs, India needing only 41.2 overs for victory)? And what about the loss to South Africa? Australia had sent South Africa in, the Proteas putting on 100 runs before the first wicket fell on their way to 7-311, then managed only 177 in reply, all out in 40.5 overs.

The Australians managed to recover to win seven games straight to reach the semi-finals where they played South Africa again. It was a different outcome this time, Australia winning by three wickets: Australia 7- 215 (Head 62, Shamsi 2-42, Coetzee 2-47); South Africa 212 (Miller 101, Klaasen 47, Starc 3-34, Hazlewood 2-12).

But the doubts remained about Australia beating warm favourites India. An Indian commentator noted: "A black soil track, rolled heavily to ensure slowness, is on offer. Batting will be difficult under the lights if the opposition has two quality spinners operating in the middle overs."

Most Australian commentators would have choked on their pakora or whatever was on the lunch menu when they heard the news.

But Cummins had taken a close look at the wicket, from the dual perspective of captain, and a pace bowler who would have to bowl on it.

It was the same wicket used in an India-Pakistan match a month earlier (India won comfortably losing only three wickets to pass Pakistan's total of 191 all out in 42.5 overs). It also would not have escaped the notice of Cummins that the three Indian pace bowlers had taken six wickets between them.

He'd recognised that the slow deck would be difficult for batting early. He also banked on the dew settling under lights to make batting easier in the second innings.

"I am not a great pitch reader, but it looked pretty firm. They have only just watered it, so yeah, (we will) give it another 24 hours and have a look. But it looks like a pretty good wicket," Cummins said. He'd read it very well.

Sharma began in dashing form, but the crowd was hushed when Gill was out for just four runs with only 30 on the board.

Kohli joined his captain and together they seemed to have the attack under control.

But Sharma had a rush of blood and was next to go when he charged down the pitch at Maxwell, lofting a miscued drive towards the extra cover boundary where Travis Head took a great catch, running back towards the boundary rope, lunging, and taking the ball over his shoulder.

ONE-DAY, SOME DAY!

It was time for some Cummins magic. He came on to have a crack at Kohli.

Cummins bowled a ball short of a good length and Kohli tried to guide it towards third man for a single. Instead, he chopped it back on to his stumps. The Indian fans were silenced as Kohli departed for 54. The only further resistance was to come from keeper KL Rahul who made 66.

India was all out in the final over for 240 runs, most previous winning scores in the tournament having surpassed that total. But if the wicket was going to play tricks when the Australians batted under lights, it could be sufficient.

Cummins took 2-34 from his 10 overs and became the first paceman in the tournament to bowl 10 overs without conceding a boundary.

Australia got off to a shaky start when Warner went for just seven, followed by Marsh for 15 and Smith for four.

Head opened the innings and made 137 from 120 balls to ensure Australia stayed alive. Labuschagne was not out 58 as he and Maxwell saw Australia safely home in the 43rd over.

Head was named Man of the Match. Adam Zampa was named in the team of the tournament for his 23 wickets.

South Africa and India had beaten Australia in the first two rounds. Australia returned serve in the finals series.

Fast bowler Mitch Starc praised his skipper for his all-round display at the tournament as a leader, and with the ball in hand.

"He (Cummins) was phenomenal," Starc said.

"I think he's been phenomenal all tournament in his leadership, his decision making. At times we've needed to step up with the ball, just been a bit flat, and he's been phenomenal for us, and this has just capped off an unbelievable eight weeks for this group."

Cummins spoke to journalists after the presentations: "I always like to say I'm pretty relaxed, but I was a little bit nervous this morning just pacing around waiting for it to get started, seeing the sea of blue in the hotel getting nearer the ground and seeing the sea of blue, walking, making its way to the ground.

"All the cars parked, people with their selfie cameras out, you kind of knew you were walking into something pretty special.

"And then to walk out for the toss and just see 130,000 blue Indian shirts, it's an experience you'll never forget.

"Awesome day, and the good thing was they weren't too noisy for most of it."

An Indian scribe wrote: "Australians played a near perfect game, and Cummins's leadership shone through. He gave overs to spinners Maxwell and Travis Head when he knew the Indians were not trying to attack, he cut off Suryakumar Yadav's favourite area behind the stumps and his pacers bowled slow bouncers to him, and he brought himself on in the middle of the innings and got Virat Kohli."

Even a leading Indian player was in awe.

Test superstar Ashwin, who made just one appearance in the World Cup, believed Cummins and Australia played the perfect game in the final as the unbeaten Indian side was left stunned.

"Cummins' execution should be applauded," Ashwin said on his YouTube channel.

"It is easy to plan to bowl to a leg-side field. It is easier to bowl that way in a Test match because the umpires will not call a wide even if you bowl a couple of balls down leg.

"But to not bowl a wide down leg in an ODI, execute the plans with that field and not allow batters to drive the ball is brilliant.

"In my experience, I have seen bowlers go for at least one or two fours with such a field. It was the first time I saw a fast bowler bowl to an offspinner's field without a mid-off in a one-day game. Tactical brilliance, tactical execution. They had us there."

The call to bowl first after winning the toss was a major surprise to many, including Ashwin who asked Australia's chairman of selectors George Bailey about it.

"Australia deceived me personally with their decision at the toss," Ashwin said.

"I was checking out if the pitch was disintegrating at the mid-innings and I met George Bailey, the chairman of selectors.

"And I asked, 'Why didn't you guys bat first like you always do after winning the toss?'

"For that, he answered back, 'We have played IPL and bilateral series for a long time now, and in our experience the red soil disintegrates but the black soil gets better to bat on under lights'."

Ashwin said Bailey told him: "In the match against South Africa at Lucknow, it was a red soil pitch that didn't just seam, but turned too as time went by.

"Dew is not a big impact on red soil pitches whereas black soil pitches are good turners in the afternoon but in the night the pitch solidifies into a flat track and plays as though it's made of concrete."

Arriving back home after six months "on the road", Cummins described winning the World Cup in a field of 10 countries as "career-defining legacy" for the team.

"I think they have created their own legacy," he said of his teammates.

"A World Cup, you only get one chance every four years and especially playing somewhere like India, it's hard.

"To be pitted up against the rest of the world and come away with a medal, it doesn't get any better than that.

"Adding to that an away-Ashes series, a World Test Championship. We couldn't have planned for much better. So a pretty satisfied group."

For Indian captain Rohit Sharma and his players, the loss was heart-breaking.

Rohit said it never "occurred" to anyone in the camp that they could lose the final.

"We were jokingly talking about it, 'oh we've been unbeaten so far…' before the final, the thought of losing never even occurred to us. We had the belief that we had been playing really good cricket, we will run through. We will keep going in the same direction," Rohit said.

"I ran (towards dressing room after the loss). I was in no mood to stay there. Honestly, I just wanted this so badly. I mean, when you want something so desperately and you're not getting it, you get frustrated. You get disappointed. You get angry, you get all these negative thoughts running through your head. At that moment, you can't even think of what's happened in life. You don't understand that. You just want to go home."

The *Hindustan Times* reported Rohit mentioned a conversation with his wife, Ritika Sajdeh, and said it took him a couple of days to come to terms with the loss. He said the final in Ahmedabad felt like a bad dream.

"Next day, when I woke up, I had no idea what had happened the night before," Rohit said. "I couldn't understand it. I was discussing it with my wife and I said, 'whatever happened last night was a bad dream, right? I think the final is tomorrow'. It took me two to three days to realise and process that, yes, we have indeed lost the World Cup. Now we have to wait another four years for another chance."

The win gave Australia its sixth World Cup; previous wins were in 1987, 1999, 2003, 2007 and 2015. The First World Cup was held in 1975 and the 2023 version was the 13th.

Cummins played his first ODI in Australia's tour of South Africa in 2011. He focussed on the short-form of the game through his rehabilitation from long-term injury, so he was no mug at the game.

Eleven years after his first ODI, he was made captain (17 November 2022) when Aaron Finch stood down.

Cummins' record at that point was 73 matches, 119 wickets at an average of 28.04 and economy of 5.21.

He had captained Australia in just four ODI games before the World Cup, the least-experienced captain in the tournament.

As for his own bowling and batting in the World Cup, he took 15 wickets in 11 matches at an economy of 5.75 and scored 128 runs in 8 innings with average of 32.

In May 2024, his overall record (since 2011) was 88 matches for 141 wickets at an average of 28.66 and economy of 5.29. He'd scored 492 runs at an average of 13.66.

ONE-DAY, SOME DAY!

SUMMARY WTC FINAL

India 240 all out in 50 overs: KL Rahul (66 off 107 balls), Virat Kohli (54 off 63), Rohit Sharma (47 off 31); Mitchell Starc (3-55), Pat Cummins (2-34), Josh Hazlewood (2-60).

Australia 4-241 in 43 overs: Travis Head (137 off 120 balls), Marnus Labuschagne (58no off 110); Jasprit Bumrah (2-43), Mohammed Siraj (1-45), Mohammed Shami (1-47).

Player of the Match: Travis Head.

5

TESTING TIMES

Pat Cummins would be challenged both as leader and strike bowler in Test matches that were to follow success in the Ashes in 2021-22 and before the return series in 2023.

In 2019 he was ranked by the ICC as the No. 1 Test bowler in world cricket. He stayed there until 2023 when he was deposed after the unsuccessful tour of India. By April 2024 he was down to No. 5, creditable, and as opposing batters would testify, still a threat with the new or "new-ish" ball in his hand.

Teammate Josh Hazelwood had risen past him to No. 2. Indian spinner Ravi Ashwin was No. 1.

Perhaps Cummins' Test bowling statistics tell a story.

In his comeback year, 2017, he played in eight Tests and took 29 wickets. He played another eight Tests in 2018, taking 44 wickets as he regained something like the level of menace he reached in South Africa seven years before.

For Cummins, 2019 was the year that convinced the cricket world that he was among the world's elite fast bowlers, the best.

He finished the year with 59 wickets at an average of 20.14. His wicket tally was 14 better than next best and the biggest by a fast bowler since (Sir) Richard Hadlee in 1985.

Cummins took 10 wickets in the 2019 Brisbane Test against Sri Lanka.

It was a good year for Australians; Cummins was one of five picked in the ICC's Test team of the year, with Steve Smith, Marnus

TESTING TIMES

Labuschagne, Mitchell Starc and Nathan Lyon.

It also was a World Cup year in ODIs – Cummins took 14 wickets in his 10 matches. Starc was the leading wicket-taker with 27 and England defeated New Zealand in the final. (India and Australia finished 1 and 2 but bowed out in the semi-finals).

Covid impacted world Test cricket (and all other forms) from 2020 to 2022. Nevertheless, those three years produced a slightly clearer picture of the captain v bowler question.

Cummins played only three Tests in 2020 for 14 wickets, and the following year he played four Tests, all as captain, and took 21 wickets, including seven wickets in his first Test at the helm.

In 2021, Cummins was a member of the Australian side that won its first T20 World Cup. He wasn't captain.

In 2022 Cummins played 10 Tests and took 36 wickets. In 2023 he played 11 Tests and took 42 wickets. In the first half of 2024 he played five Tests and took 17 wickets (Australia was scheduled to play nine Tests in 2024).

When the quality of the opposition and the fact that Cummins turned 30 in 2023 is considered, his record in 2022-23 doesn't seem to indicate his bowling skill dropped significantly. It must also be noted that Nathan Lyon was still taking bags of wickets and Josh Hazlewood had come into his own in the pace department where he, his captain and Mitchell Starc comprised one of the most formidable pace attacks in the game.

After just more than three years, captaincy had become Cummins' forte and by 2024 his mark was confirmed as an A-plus. The trophy cabinet was impressive, including two world championships.

Waiting for the Australians after their Ashes success in 2021-22 was Pakistan in a first visit there since 1998 when Australia won the three-Test series 1-0.

After that came a two-Test series in Sri Lanka.

The Australians wouldn't play at home until November-December 2022 when the West Indies visited.

The Christmas-New Year saw Australia host South Africa for three Tests.

Then it was off to India in February 2023 for one of their biggest challenges since the Ashes in 2021-22.

• • •

Cummins led the team in four of the five Ashes matches in 2021-22 that saw Australia rise to the top of the Tests pointscore, winning three of the Tests against England by big margins.

The team fell just one wicket short of doing the same in the other Test and despite missing a match through no fault of his own he took more wickets than any other bowler from either side.

Just two months after the Ashes triumph at home – March 2022 – Cummins was leading his team on an historic tour of Pakistan, the first by Australia for 24 years. He was a winner again, Australia claiming the three-match series 1-0.

The first two matches in Pakistan were on pitches that gave little help to bowlers. Draws were predictable.

In the second Test Australia had reached 8-503 when Alex Carey was out for 93 late on the second day. That looked like enough to declare and have a shot at the Pakistan openers.

But Cummins could see the wicket was a batter's paradise and suspected that such a massive total might not be enough.

So he padded up and saw out the remaining overs, only to resume again next day. He, Starc and Swepson pushed on to reach 9-556 before calling a halt. Cummins remained 36 not out.

The total probably was enough to ensure Australia wasn't beaten if nothing else. The pitch looked like it might break up late in the match but could yield a lot of runs in the meantime.

But in Pakistan's turn at the wicket, Australia's bowlers turned down the screws to dismiss the home side for 148, a surprisingly low score.

Probably mindful of the runs that could be scored despite Pakistan's capitulation, Cummins batted again, adding a further 92 runs for the

TESTING TIMES

loss of two wickets before declaring.

Australia had a real fighting chance of victory, but all the fight came from Pakistan, Shafique making 96, skipper Azam 196 and keeper Rizwan 104 to reach 7-443 at the close to orchestrate a draw, three wickets in hand and 57 runs short. Cummins was right in his guess that there were plenty of runs to be had.

Inevitably the question was asked why Australia didn't declare earlier. After both sides completed their first innings, Australia led by 408 runs. To bat on or to declare?

A declaration on 556 could have meant Australia had to bat again anyway, possibly on a crumbling wicket – any lead by Pakistan might have put Australia under pressure in a run chase. Time needed was the unknown factor in that equation.

A draw was not a bad outcome. Australia led the series 1-0 with the third Test to come.

Cummins was determined to get a result in the third Test at Lahore to seal the Benaud-Qadar Trophy.

He did that by making a generous declaration late on the fourth day, setting Pakistan a potentially gettable 351 off 121 overs, under three an over. Despite a strong start – the Pakistanis still had 10 wickets in hand, needing 278 off 90 overs when the final day began – they were bowled out 151 runs short of the target. Again, Cummins' enterprising and confident captaincy had triumphed.

Cummins: "It was an amazing experience, a lot of fun. We are elated."

As it turned out, the Pakistan strips for the March series suited the batters – the bowlers didn't have a lot of joy as the two teams scored a total 3,551 runs, averaging more than 1,000 runs per Test.

Cummins took 12 wickets for 270.

Cummins, fellow fast bowlers Mitchell Starc and Josh Hazlewood, and Glenn Maxwell were left out of the 16-man squad for the ODI series that followed and was won 2-1 by the home team. Australia won the sole T20 match.

Next stop was Sri Lanka in June against a home side that had been languishing down the table of Test cricket rankings since 2016 when they had a comprehensive 3-0 series win over Australia on home turf.

Sri Lanka at home again in June-July 2022 presented a challenge for Australia that was not taken likely. Nevertheless, Australia won the first Test, in Galle, by 10 wickets.

The second Test of two, saw Sri Lanka humble Australia by an innings and 39 runs. What happened?

Australia batted after winning the toss and the first innings of 364 seemed decent.

When it came to bowling Sri Lanka out, Australia found the going hard, the Sri Lankans making 554. Cummins toiled hard for his 1-95 from 30 overs.

Australia capitulated in the second innings, all out for 151, lasting less than four hours trying to save the match against the devastating Sri Lankan spin attack. The series was drawn 1-1.

Cummins saw the series as a solid preparation for the looming tour of India.

"Some batters went out with a really clear plan, and you just get a ball with your name on it earlier than you would've liked," he said. "It's a good reality check for people touring over here that it's really hard. So many positives out of last week, that we did find methods that work. One small hiccup doesn't mean you have to change everything. And it makes for more learning than after a win.

"I think half our batting line-up and half our bowling line-up hasn't played a lot over here in the sub-continent. So the experience on these two vastly different wickets, I think we got a lot of lessons out of it to take to India."

Sri Lanka won the five-match ODI series 3-2, and Australia won the three-match T20 series 2-1. Cummins played in four of the ODIs, taking eight wickets. He didn't play in the T20 series.

Returning to Australia, the next assignment was a two-Test series in November-December against the West Indies, another side that was down the lower end of the Test rankings.

TESTING TIMES

There was no slacking off for the Australians who took the series 2-0, winning by 164 runs and 419 runs respectively.

It was a quick turnaround to the next series, three Tests at home against South Africa, including a traditional Boxing Day match at the Melbourne Cricket Ground.

Again, there was no slacking off, Australia winning the series 2-0, by six wickets in Brisbane and by an innings and 182 runs at the MCG. The Sydney Test in January 2023 was drawn.

The Gabba ground in Brisbane was sanctioned by the ICC, receiving a "below average" rating and one demerit point from match referee Richie Richardson, after the Test was over within two days, only the second time that had happened (the first was in 1931).

The highlights of such a brief match were Mitchell Starc taking his 300th Test wicket and Travis Head passing 2,000 Test runs.

Australia had a comfortable victory in the Boxing Day Test in Melbourne, even though a session's play was lost to weather. Australia won by an innings and 182 runs.

David Warner in his 100th Test passed 8,000 runs with a double century.

The Third Test, in Sydney, was drawn. More than a day was lost to rain, but Steve Smith managed to score his 30th Test century, equal third most among Australians.

Cummins took the most wickets in the series – 12.

At last, in February-March, the eagerly awaited tour to India was upon the Australians. Revenge was a priority, after Australia lost the most recent contests, both at home, in 2018-19 (India's first series victory in Australia) and 2020-21.

Cummins picked up 14 wickets at 27.78 in 2018-19, but it wasn't enough to stop India piling on the runs, 7-443 and 7-662 in the Melbourne and Sydney Tests respectively on the way to a 2-1 series win.

Cummins believed he'd become a better bowler for the experience. "There were a few lessons," he said. "The first lesson I learnt was how brutal Test cricket is. They might bat all of day one and there's nothing that'll stop them batting of day two unless we take wickets, which they did a few times. They showed us what you have to be, what level you have to be at, to be the best team in the world."

India must have learned something about playing Test cricket in Australia, too, as their return just two seasons later (2020-21) produced the same result, a 2-1 win for the visitors. Tim Paine was Australian captain then.

Cummins had done a creditable job as the spearhead of the attack, finishing the series with 21 wickets for 421 runs, taking four wickets three times.

The Border-Gavaskar Trophy rematch in India over four Tests in February-March 2023 was highly anticipated, particularly with Cummins now leading the team and the two countries ranked 1 and 2 in Test cricket by the ICC.

The sub-continent, India in particular, had not been a particularly happy hunting ground, and the Australians' chances would depend a lot on how they coped with the slower wickets that usually didn't suit the likes of Cummins, Hazlewood and Starc.

Australia needed to be bold.

In the 28 Test series between the two countries since 1947-48, Australia had won only 12, their last in India in 2004-05.

Spinner Todd Murphy was included in Australia's squad, joining Ashton Agar and Mitchell Swepson as options to support frontline spinner Nathan Lyon on the slow, turning wickets that were expected.

Cummins had plenty to think about as his team arrived in India, not just the cricket. He left with the team aware that his mother Maria was seriously ill. Her health deteriorated rapidly and Cummins left the tour after the first two Tests to be with his family for his mother's last days.

The cricket didn't begin well in Nagpur.

Australia's total of 177 was never likely to be enough, no batter making a half-century. Eight wickets fell to the spin of Jadeja and Ashwin.

India replied with 400, captain Rohit Sharma making 120.

Needing just 224 to make India bat again, Australia capitulated, all

TESTING TIMES

out for 91, Smith's 25 the best. Ashwin and man-of-the match Jadeja took seven wickets as India won by an innings and 132.

The second Test at Delhi saw Australia lead on the first innings, by the narrowest margin, before the batters failed again in the second. Australia made 263 thanks to Khawaja and Handscomb. India replied with 262, the spinners led by Lyon sharing nine wickets.

Australia made only 113 in the second innings, no batter making a half-century. Ashwin and Jadeja claimed all 10 wickets.

India lost four wickets getting 118 for victory and a 2-0 lead in the series.

Could Australia turn things around, without their captain?

The third Test, at Indore didn't produce a run-feast, but it did see Australia get a victory.

India batted first and made only 109, spinners Kuhnemann, Lyon and Murphy sharing nine wickets.

Australia replied with 197, Khawaja's 60 the best. Yet again it was Ashwin and Jadeja the destroyers, sharing seven wickets.

India made 163 in their second innings; Lyon claimed eight wickets in one of his best bowling performances. Australia lost only one wicket in reaching 78 to win the Test and keep interest in the series alive.

The fourth Test, in Ahmedabad, saw runs aplenty but no result.

Australia made 480 (Khawaja 180, Green 114) to at last put pressure on the Indian attack, although spin again produced most wickets for the home side.

India also found batting conditions to their liking and made 571 to make an Australian win extremely unlikely. Gill and Kohli made centuries and Australia's spinners copped a bit of stick but took seven wickets.

Australia was 2-175 in their second innings at the close of the match. The draw left Australia losing the series 2-1.

There was no redemption for Australia against India this time.

An upside however was that Australia's one win gave them enough points to get into the World Test Championship final, against India again, three months later, in neutral territory, at The Oval, England. And they'd have their skipper back.

• • •

Pakistan was back in Australia for three Tests at the end of 2023. Australia won the first Test, in Perth, by 360 runs. Warner made 164 and Mitch Marsh 90 in a first innings total of 487. Khawaja made 90 in the second innings. Lyon had match figures of 5-80.

Australia won the Boxing Day Test in Melbourne by 79 runs. Pat Cummins had match figures of 10 for 97, five wickets in each innings.

Australia sealed the series with an eight-wickets win in the Sydney Test where Cummins had match figures of 6-85.

After that series ended the Australians were on their way to New Zealand for two Tests in February 2024. They won both, by 172 runs then three wickets respectively. Nathan Lyon took 10 wickets in the first Test and in a rare "miss" Cummins didn't take a wicket in the home side's second innings.

In the second Test, Cummins made 23 runs and 32 not out to go with his five wickets for the match.

That completed seven successive Tests in quick time for the Australians. Testing times indeed.

An upside was that fewer Tests were going the full distance. That would have been a great relief to the bowlers who by now were all in their 30s – Nathan Lyon 36, Mitchell Starc 34 and Josh Hazlewood 33. Cummins was the "pup" at 30.

The Test cricket Cummins first experienced in his early days was much more of a grind and he pointed out that the shorter versions seen in the 2020s (not by design, mind you, it was just how things panned out) was the reason the four front-line members of the Australian attack were able to play all five Tests in the 2023-24 summer just completed.

Lyon ("The GOAT") had 517 career wickets, Starc had 353 and Hazlewood and Cummins each had 263.

Retirement looming? "We've not spoken about it at all," said Lyon.

6

SHORT AND SWEET

Cricket fans accepted the one-day format of cricket willingly, enthusiastically in some parts of the world. A match that was over in one day had appeal.

There were fears about the future of Test cricket amid the rising number of short-form matches.

Watching a full Test match required spectators to find up to five successive days of free time, to either go to the full match or watch on TV.

There would be no way fans in the 21st Century would cop a Test match that went 11 days, as did the "The Timeless Test" between England and South Africa at Durban in 1939. It was eventually abandoned as a draw after nine days of play spread over 12 days. The England team had to catch the boat home, after all.

Modern Test cricket is confined to five days, thankfully. That has been the case since 1979, with one exception: the Super Test between Australia and the Rest of the World in 2005 that was scheduled for the SCG over six days but finished in three-and-a-half (Australia winning by 110 runs).

Not many Tests last five days now and those that do usually have had a weather interruption. The regulation says: "Test matches shall be of five days scheduled duration."

The International Cricket Council (ICC) in 2017 raised the possibility that after 2023 Tests could be cut to four days. There's been no change yet with a belief now that ODIs and T20 internationals satisfy the needs of those who want a quick result. The prevalence of those games and other short-forms does however put scheduling of all cricket under some stress, particularly with the Cups in those short forms.

• • •

The rise of franchise cricket has poured large amounts of money into the pockets of cricketers. World Series Cricket did likewise but not to the same extent, as far as we know now.

World Series Cricket challenged the cricket establishment. Is franchise cricket doing the same?

For more than a century, young cricketers have dreamt of playing for their country. They would have been thinking Test cricket, Don Bradman No. 1 on the list of those they'd like to emulate.

Years later there was Dennis Lillee, then Shane Warne. Their statues stand outside the MCG. Every cricket fan had a hero and those two have been top of the list in Australia.

Which youngster didn't have a cricket bat and a dream? There was genuine love for the game. Money only really became "a thing" when World Series Cricket came on the scene.

What is the case today?

The lucrative franchise leagues around the world seem to have put money in the forefront of the minds of young cricketers. An IPL contract for the lucky handful can be worth several times more than a Cricket Australia one.

Test cricket has been on decline in some traditional Test-playing countries. The West Indies, once a powerhouse in world cricket now struggles to field competitive Test teams. Yet West Indian players can be seen in many of the franchise leagues.

For the "big three" in Test cricket, India, England and Australia, Test cricket still brings in tidy sums. And their players get contracts that are well-worth having. Many Test players also supplement their income with short-term contracts in the T20 leagues.

That sometimes causes friction with their "parent" cricket boards, but most players so far have managed the juggling act between representing their country and playing for the "big bucks" in a T20 league.

Some players have opted to concentrate solely on the money leagues, forsaking national representation, particularly if playing for their country comes at a price rather than a profit.

A report in August 2023 referred to New Zealand bowler Trent Boult, the fourth-highest wicket-taker in New Zealand cricket. He reportedly opted for an early retirement from national duty to play franchise cricket. Spending more time with his family was a contributing factor, too. He was 33 when he made his call in 2022.

Players can't be criticised for taking the franchise option. Cricket for many now is a full-time job with a lot of travel, and full-time jobs warrant reasonable reward.

Imagine how players who stick with their national contracts feel when they see the money being bandied about at the IPL pre-season auction of players, for example.

It seems highly unlikely that Test-playing nations will be able to offer their players those sorts of sums and their ruling bodies would be hoping that Test cricket will survive alongside the burgeoning short-form leagues.

As of June 2024, 28 countries held T20 leagues, not all of them open to international players on big pay.

T20 will continue to grow. It is embraced by younger fans, TV networks and players.

The debate comes down to what the players want and what the fans want to see. They may not be the same things.

Can Test cricket, particularly the Ashes, survive? Should it?

PAT CUMMINS

RON REED: IN SUPPORT OF TEST CRICKET

I've been hooked on cricket in general, and the Ashes in particular, all my longish life, a very large part of which has been spent writing about it professionally and watching it for pleasure.

Yes, of course I'd enjoy five lots of five days of hard-fought combat, ending 3-2 but you know what — such a scoreline has only ever occurred six times, and three of those date back almost 120 years.

So it doesn't necessarily have to be a nail-biter to be entertaining. There is always plenty of drama, memorable stories unfold, reputations are made and unmade, record books — and no sport so loves facts and figures more than cricket — are rewritten and expanded.

Along with its great sense of history and tradition, one of the concept's powerful strengths — in my opinion, which is not universally shared — is that it is played over five matches, which is no longer the case in any other match-up with or between any other countries.

Whether it is taking place in England or Australia, that means there is ample scope for subtly different playing conditions to be explored, for strategies to be devised and tested, for players to work their way into and out of form, for new stars to emerge and fading ones to be farewelled, for a narrative to fully unfold, and for fans in almost every part of the country to get the chance to witness it in person.

In other ways cricket has embraced a "less is more" philosophy, which is why white ball formats, especially T20, have been so successful, certainly their World Cups—but it would be a mistake to translate that thinking to the Ashes

From *Captain Pat: Cometh the Hour, Cummins the Man*

SHORT AND SWEET

Pat Cummins believes the decline of long-format cricket isn't as dramatic as some people had been painting it to be.

"My hopes are that it's even stronger than it is now, in ten years' time or 20 years' time," he said in Sydney before the Pakistan Test in 2024.

Crowd numbers for the recent Pakistan and West Indies Tests raised some questions.

"I think in some regards leading to this Test summer, some of the question marks were against Pakistan and West Indies. We've had two fantastic Test matches against Pakistan, really well supported, big crowds," Cummins said.

"So I don't think it's in as dramatic a decline as sometimes it gets spoken about. But I think there is an issue just with the amount of other cricket out there, obviously competition for talent is higher than it's ever been."

Cummins has been something of a regular player (on big money) in the IPL. He does have Cricket Australia's most lucrative contract, befitting the national captain.

He likes to put national duty first. That was the case in 2023 when he decided to bypass the IPL.

He recognised that a packed international schedule in 2023 that included a tour to India, an Ashes and the ODI World Cup required his undivided attention as captain of Australia.

"I've made the difficult decision to miss next year's IPL," he said in late 2022.

"The international schedule is packed with Tests and ODIs for the next 12 months, so I will take some rest ahead of an Ashes series and World Cup."

Australian cricket fans were extremely pleased he did.

• • •

The 50-overs game gained traction with television audiences from the 1970s thanks to Australian Kerry Packer, head of the Nine Network at the time, and his World Series Cricket. Innovations included coloured clothing and a white ball at night. And let's not forget Tony Greig's crash helmet, though it (and the player under it) may have become a target for some aggressive bowling sometimes as a result of its presence.

One-day games appealed to TV network executives because they could slot in the broadcasts around other programming over a week, particularly the much-loved "soapies".

A full day of cricket, however, was problematic for some spectators if it was played during the working week. An innovation became day-night games of 50 overs that allowed the nine-to-fivers to get their cricket "fix" after work.

T20 games in Australia are now almost exclusively played under lights and have proved a hit with fans, even school-age ones who may have to be up early next day for their education "fix".

A further shortened form of cricket known as Cricket Max was developed in New Zealand in 1996 by former Test batsman Martin Crowe. Club cricket had been playing short versions of cricket, such as double-wicket (two-player) competitions for years, often as charity or social matches. Cricket Max was a whole new competitive concept.

Crowe explained the introduction of his game: "I invented and designed Cricket Max because I felt it was time to provide to our spectators and TV viewers a game of cricket that was short in duration, very colourful, kept some old traditions and highlighted the best skills in the game.

"After 15 years of one-day cricket I could see a need for a new visual appeal in terms of the field lay-out, and the rules. This will provide great entertainment and an exciting result in three hours of cricket. There is far more scoring than ever before, also the potential for electric defensive work in the field. Cricket Max can be played and watched by anyone, but nothing can beat seeing the best in the world display their skills in a whole match in just three hours."

Crowe's point wasn't lost on cricket administrators.

England and Wales Cricket Board (ECB) marketing executive Stuart

SHORT AND SWEET

Robertson saw a much-shortened version of cricket as being an answer to declining attendances at County matches in the UK.

It should be noted cricket officials didn't stop at 20 overs – in 2017 the first competition of T10 or 10-10 cricket was held in the United Arab Emirates, and officially sanctioned by the International Cricket Council (ICC).

As the name suggests, each team bowls 10 overs and a game takes around 90 minutes. T-10 leagues are appearing several countries, particularly among non-Test playing ones. It has been suggested the format could some day be included in Olympic Games.

Cricket Max was played over four quarters with innings split into two sets of 10 eight-ball overs and ran for seven years in New Zealand.

A new variation to the short-form game is The Hundred, introduced by the England and Wales Cricket Board (ECB) in 2021. As the name suggests each team bowls 100 balls. Each bowler gets a maximum of 20 balls that can be bowled in four spells of 5 or two spells of 10, rather than 6-ball overs. Bowling ends are swapped after 10 balls. There's no drinks break and a maximum of 15 minutes between innings.

Remaining rules are similar to those in T20.

The Hundred features eight teams across seven cities, a similar basis to the IPL.

Teams play against each other home-and-away in the group stage of 32 matches. Whichever team finishes top goes to the final while second and third face off in a single eliminator match to determine the other finalist.

In 2024, the ECB decided to allow the establishment of franchises via private investment by the 2025 season.

Australians Adam Zampa and Spencer Johnson played in The Hundred for 2023 winners The Oval Invincibles and were retained for the 2024 edition. Johnson took 3-1 off his 20 balls against the Manchester Originals in a game in 2023.

Both were also going to be involved in the overlapping Major League Cricket season in the US with the Los Angeles Knight Riders.

PAT CUMMINS

Other Australians signed for The Hundred to be played in 2024 included Nathan Ellis and Matt Short. At least 10 Australian men and half a dozen women have played in the competitions since they began.

The women's competition included Australians Ellyse Perry, Grace Harris, Phoebe Litchfield, Georgia Wareham and Alana King.

Pat Cummins had not played in The Hundred.

The timing of the competition caused some angst within India's IPL management when English players were called home before the IPL play-offs.

The Hundred is played in a double-header format, two matches on the same ground, each no longer than 2.5 hours.

Other variations of short-form cricket include 90 overs and six-a-side games.

All these leagues have to be compressed into an extremely tight year-round schedule.

ESPNcricinfo's *Cricket Monthly* published this summary in 2018 in its first survey of cricketers and their workloads: "South Africa's Dane Vilas is the world's most-playing cricketer. Jonny Bairstow and Joe Root are engaged in an international match every fourth day of the year. Virat Kohli faces more balls than anyone else in the business. Jeetan Patel bowls the most balls. And Rashid Khan is the planet's most prolific T20 cricketer, as well as its widest traveller."

Three players have played more than 100 games across the three formats of international cricket. New Zealander Ross Taylor was first. He was joined by Virat Kohli and David Warner.

• • •

T20 cricket remains the most common short form. The ECB drew up rules and the first tournament was played by English county teams in 2003.

T20 gained traction in domestic competitions and went international on 17 February 2005, when Australia and New Zealand faced off.

SHORT AND SWEET

T20 cricket then took its place on the international cricket schedule, including the first World Cup which was played in South Africa in 2007, won by India.

T20 matches are renowned for being batter-friendly. Pure cricket shots are not always the norm, and there's also a fair bit of outright slogging. "Cow corner" has become a popular place to hit the ball; reverse sweeps and lap-shots are used to great effect by proficient batters, such as Australia's Glenn Maxwell. Bowlers can expect a hammering as lights flash, flames light the night sky, electronic scoreboards record the number of sixes and crowds go wild as soon as a batter makes contact. A good number of spare balls has to be on hand as some of those that disappear over fences into the darkness do not return.

Pat Cummins said during the 2024 IPL series in India that as a bowler if you went for fewer than 10 runs an over you had done well.

Asked about how bowlers dealt with the onslaught, Cummins said: "It gets harder and harder. With the scores getting a lot bigger, you can have some games where it's quite brutal for you as a bowler. You've got to really pick yourself up and bounce back quickly. But it also does present some opportunities where you might bowl an over at the end where the team needs 15 runs in an over; if you bowl an over that goes for seven or eight at this stage, that's not just an average over, that's a match-winning over. So I think you've got to reframe it and see each over and each ball as an opportunity to try and make a difference, even if it does feel like the odds are stacked up against you sometimes."

Asked about the difference in captaincy in T20 compared to long forms, Cummins agreed a significant adjustment was required, the short form was more frantic.

"It certainly is an adjustment," he said. "I think because I've done it quite often over the years, you do get a little bit better at it. You develop a kind of confidence, that once you step onto the field, you'll be able to figure the pace out a little bit better. In T20, you've got 24 balls to try and make an impact. With Test cricket, it's over five days, so you have to pace yourself a little bit more."

Sunrisers Hyderabad (SRH) finished last in the IPL in 2023 and chose Cummins as the best prospect of leading them back to glory. New Zealander Daniel Vettori was recruited as coach (from his job as assistant coach of Australia) and the pair effected a stunning turnaround in fortunes that included three 260-plus totals in the first half of the season; one of those scores was a highest IPL score of 2-287. SRH went on to contest the IPL final.

Power-hitting was the name of the game, but SRH wasn't alone in that respect.

Bowlers were taken to the cleaners in several matches, but Cummins recognised that aggression from batters was the key to the game.

In an interview with the *Times of India* during IPL 2024, he was asked about leading an IPL side.

"I have not captained in T20 cricket or the IPL. I was excited to work alongside Daniel Vettori as coach," he said. "I didn't know many of the Sunrisers players or staff but they've been amazing.

"I didn't have any baggage because I wasn't here for the past two years.

"For us it was about committing to a style…about how we wanted to play, a style we thought would give us the best chance of winning, and that has been to be really aggressive with the bat. Travis Head epitomises how we want to play and that is to go and play with freedom."

Sounds a bit like Bazball.

Was it a bad time to be a bowler or captain in the IPL?

"Yeah, it feels like a bit of a shift in T20 cricket now," Cummins said. "Even five years ago, under eight an over was the aim. Now if you're bowling some death overs or in the powerplay, if you go under 10 an over that feels like a good day. So, it's just readjusting your own expectations and knowing that even if you bowl an over for eight or nine, that could be match-winning at the right time."

As if to emphasise his point, Cummins led the Sunrisers Hyderabad to a thrilling one-run victory over top-of-the-table Rajasthan Royals in the first week of May 2024. SRH made 201 and the Royals looked to have every chance of chasing down the total, always close to the run-rate of 10 an over that was required.

Cummins's first two overs yielded two wickets but at a cost of around 20 runs. He needed to step up. He bowled the 15th over and conceded only three runs. He bowled the second last over and conceded eight runs. The Royals had wickets in hand but were under great pressure as the required run-rate crept up. It came down to the last ball. An lbw decision gave SRH the win.

Cummins used seven bowlers but only he and left-arm paceman Natarajan kept their figures below 10 runs an over.

Just as each cricket-playing country developed its own 50-over competition, T20 cricket also found a place in domestic schedules and a Champions League competition between the best club sides from around the world — similar to that contested in European football — is held at the end of each T20 season.

Reluctant at first to embrace the idea, India when it got involved did so in a big way, with its Indian Premier League, to the extent that in 2024, 72 players (30 from overseas) were bought at auction for a total of around A$43 million by the 10 city-based franchises.

The IPL provides countries with a lot of data that can be used in selecting their national teams for tournaments such as the World T20 Cup. Many IPL players are professionals in the short game, travelling from league to league throughout the year, and not seen in longer forms.

In 2024, 17 Australians were signed to IPL teams, including Test captain Pat Cummins. Injury pre-season to Jason Behrendorff reduced Australia's contingent to 16.

The Australians would have been hoping to get into form with an eye on selection in the squad for the 2024 World Cup to be held in the Americas (hosted by the West Indies and the US). The World Cup (the ninth) comprised 20 teams and 55 games.

One Australian who raised his hand while playing in the IPL was young Victorian Jake Fraser-McGurk. He wasn't bought at auction originally but was drafted by the Delhi Capitals after the competition began, replacing injured South African fast bowler Lungi Ngidi.

Fraser-McGurk isn't a recognised bowler, but he showed what he could do with the bat immediately he stepped out in India.

He played his first T20 premier league game in the UAE in January 24. He played twice for Australia against the West Indies in February. On his arrival in India, he warmed the bench for the first few matches. When he got his chance, he didn't waste it.

A failure by another Australian, David Warner, for just eight runs in four overs, saw coach Ricky Ponting send the youngster (he'd just turned 22) in to face the music.

But it was Fraser-McGurk calling the tune. He sent the second ball he faced into the stands.

After five IPL matches, he was averaging almost 50 runs for each time at the crease.

The word was that he would most likely be on the plane to the West Indies and the US with the Australian squad for the T20 World Cup.

It wasn't to be, selectors preferring the now-veteran David Warner as the team's strike weapon. Test vice-captain Steve Smith wasn't selected either. And despite good reviews of his captaincy at the Hyderabad Sunrisers in the IPL, Pat Cummins wasn't named as Australia's captain, Mitch Marsh retaining the job after series against South Africa, the West Indies and New Zealand.

Would that be uncomfortable? The Test captain and a T20 captain in the same side? Most likely not. Cummins seemed to like the idea of not having to call the shots on every ball, something that seems necessary in T20. He would be happy being "one of the team."

"I love it," he said in New Zealand early in the year when Marsh was captain. "Go and hide on the boundary, haven't fielded on the boundary for a while, just concentrate on bowling and nothing else."

Both Marsh and Warner had their IPL appearances in 2024 cut short by injuries, needing to regain full fitness in time for the World Cup.

SHORT AND SWEET

The US became the latest country to establish a T20 league in July 2023 with its six-team Major League Cricket. Australians Aaron Finch, Marcus Stoinis and Mitch Marsh played in the inaugural season.

In Australia, a T20 competition began in the summer of 2005-06 as a State v State competition.

Victoria won four of the first five domestic T20 tournaments.

Pat Cummins played his first T20 match for NSW in the state-based competition in January 2010 as 17-year-old, against Tasmania. He took three wickets but didn't bat.

The short form wasn't considered ideal for pace bowlers as lusty swings of the bat at fast deliveries could find edges that ran away to boundaries. Even today some teams will open an innings with a spin attack. Improvements to fielding standards were a noticeable change.

Cummins played six matches for the NSW Blues, snaring 11 wickets and regularly bowling at speeds above 145 km/h.

The tournament became known as the Big Bash, probably an indication that batting was the main attraction. But Pat Cummins had a stellar season with the ball in 2011-12, his 11 wickets the best in the league.

Cummins recalled: "It was the last season of the old Big Bash before it became the Big Bash League. Those six months were crazy. I finished school, signed up for university, debuted in 1st Grade cricket and, in the space of a couple of months, I played for New South Wales Second XI and then into the New South Wales side, and then was handed a Cricket Australia contract.

"It was a pretty turbulent few months. My whole world was accelerated and turned upside down. Suddenly, I went from being a school student to a professional cricketer.

"I just remember loving it. Stuart Clark was our New South Wales captain…and Simon Katich…guys that I obviously didn't know personally but guys I grew up watching play Test cricket. Suddenly I'm lining up with Sarfraz (Stuart Clark) at mid-off and I'm asking him where I should bowl."

His performance in the Big Bash got the further attention of the State selectors and he was called up to the NSW one-day squad. Three days after making his debut there, he was called into the NSW Sheffield Shield squad.

Many cricketers find it hard to play all three – or even sometimes more – formats of cricket in the one season. It is particularly hard on fast bowlers who have to steam in for their four overs in T20 and then perhaps bowl for two or three sessions in a day for a couple of days of a Test Match.

The result is that many national T20 teams look vastly different to the Test versions.

• • •

Pat Cummins played his first T20 game for Australia in South Africa on 13 October 2011.

His record in T20 is impressive, averaging slightly better than a wicket a match.

He played 52 T20 matches for Australia from 2011 to the end of the 2023-24 season but had not captained the side in the format.

He had bowled 190 overs in T20Is, taking 57 wickets at an average of 24.77, and economy rate of 7.45, and a strike rate of 20.

With the IPL season out of the way, the 2024 T20 World Cup was on his mind.

Australia had won only one T20 world Cup, defeating New Zealand in the final in 2021.

Rather than reducing a workload that involved commitments in all three now-regular formats of cricket, Cummins said he was determined to feature in the short-form World Cup in the USA and West Indies in 2024.

Up for grabs was the chance for Australia to be world champions in all three forms of international cricket at the one time. Australia fell well short of that ambition when bundled out of the T20 World Cup before the semi-finals. Fielding errors plagued Australia's campaign throughout – six chances were put down in the game against Scotland (the most ever in a T20 World Cup) and five against Afghanistan – a record far short of Australia's usual standards in a format where sharp fielding is so vital.

Coming on top of some fielding lapses in Test matches (five catches put down in the drawn Ashes Test in England) it appeared some work on fielding would be in order.

Although Mitchell Marsh was Australia's T20 incumbent captain it would not be impossible for Cummins to assume that role sometime soon in light of the experience he would have gained leading Hyderabad Sunrisers through the IPL. He would also have advanced his education about bowling in T20 matches.

Cummins replaced retired Aaron Finch as captain of Australia's ODI team in October 2022. Finch has since seen how Cummins has developed as a leader in the short forms of the game and gave his thoughts in an interview in India.

"Whether it's a World Cup, whether it's the Big Bash, or any other T20 competition, you sit down and you map out how you think you're going to win it," Finch said. "And you have to be prepared because it's so volatile. From Australia's point of view and SRH's too, Pat has been a wonderful leader.

"I think the calmness that he brings to a group and also being a bowler, he can sympathise with a bowler when it's not going well. He knows what to say at the right time.

"And I know in my experience as a batsman, when you speak to bowlers, sometimes you don't have the same understanding of why did you bowl that ball at that stage.

"And there's more to it than just a poorly executed delivery or maybe the plan was wrong. So, I think Pat's got that great understanding of what it takes to be a bowler in that situation. So, he gets through to them a lot easier," Finch said.

Finch said Australian cricket was mindful of the load on Pat Cummins as a player and as a leader. "It's incredibly time-consuming to be a captain of an international team and a franchise for that matter," he said.

"So, the fact that he's doing Test cricket, ODI cricket, IPL, that's an incredible load as well as playing three formats of the game and expecting to be at your absolute best day in, day out, which he has been for the last couple of years."

Australia was scheduled for a limited overs series (three T20s and five ODIs) in England in September 2024 before hosting visits by Pakistan and India at the end of the year. Cummins was not included in the white-ball squad for the England tour, resting for the Test series ahead. Marsh would be the captain in the ODIs and T20s.

Australia hosted the T20 world Cup for the first time in 2022, the eighth version of the tournament that's held every two years. England defeated Pakistan in the final. Australia was runner up to England in the 2010 final in the West Indies.

In an era when T20 appears to be designed to produce big-hitting and unconventional shots, it is a little surprising to note the performances of Australia's bowlers in the international short form.

Leading the way in the run-up to the T20 World Cup in 2024 were spinners Ashton Agar and Adam Zampa. Agar: 32 matches, 38 wickets at an average 19.53. Zampa: 41 matches, 43 wickets at an average 22.67.

Kane Richardson was best of the quicks: 26 matches for 29 wickets at an average of 24.31. Mitchell Starc: 35 matches for 47 wickets at an average of 19.38; Pat Cummins: 30 matches for 37 wickets at an average of 20.62.

FOOTNOTE: There have been nine hat-tricks in T20 World Cup matches; the first was Australian Brett Lee's in the first version of the event in 2007.

7
G-WIZ

Australian bowlers always expect to do well at Melbourne Cricket Ground Test matches – the famous and iconic ground beloved by Melbournians, the G.

Tests there usually start on Boxing Day, mostly before a near full-house – from 60,000 to 100,000 people depending on the pulling-power of the opposition.

Pat Cummins has done well at the G. In December 2023 he claimed his 250th Test wicket there and grabbed a 10-wicket haul against Pakistan.

Surprisingly, Cummins is not against moving the traditional Boxing Day Test away from the MCG – with a proviso that the move "enhances the game." The same would apply to moving the New Year's Test from Sydney.

"I think the way that Test summer works is always pretty good, but if anyone has any out-there ideas that's going to attract more fans to watch on TV or at the ground, then I think that's a good thing," Cummins said.

"Head office, obviously, look after all the scheduling, and we're pretty happy to go along with whatever is happening."

The Melbourne wicket usually has been good for fast bowling early, with spinners coming into their own later, probably the ideal traditional Test wicket.

Pat Cummins took 10 wickets in the 2023 Boxing Day Test. He was pleased the wicket was receptive to pace bowling.

He was awarded the Jonny Mullagh Medal as the leading player in the Test (5-48, 5-49), spearheading the 79-run victory over Pakistan just inside four days.

"Really happy for a few reasons," Cummins said. "The main reason is that's the best I've felt like I bowled for a little while.

"The rhythm felt really good, I felt like I had good pace."

He also claimed his 250th wicket in his 57th Test. The only other quicks to take 250 wickets in fewer Tests were Dennis Lillee and Glenn McGrath.

Cummins has played Test cricket at 29 grounds since his career began at the Wanderers Stadium in South Africa in 2011.

He has played seven Tests at each of Brisbane (the Gabba), Sydney (SCG) and Melbourne (MCG).

He has scored most runs at the MCG, 169 at an average of 17. But of course, bowling is his strength and he has taken most wickets, 40, at the Gabba on a pitch that was renowned for usually being a bit lively and well-capable of being exploited by pace bowlers.

The MCG didn't always have "juice", but Cummins had taken 63 wickets there by 2024. His 10-wicket hauls for a match came at the Gabba and the MCG.

One of the best balls he has bowled in Test cricket, if anyone would be brave enough to nominate just one from the 2,100+ overs he has sent down, could well be the one he served up to Pakistan's Babar Azam on day two of the Boxing Day Test in 2023.

Pakistan won the toss and sent Australia in. A first innings total of 318 probably wasn't a par score, but it was a target to which the Australia bowlers could work. Labuschagne was best for Australia with 63. Cummins made 13.

Pakistan was 2-124 when Babar Azam joined his skipper Shan Masood at the wicket and a first innings lead looked likely.

Babar had probably already seen the stunning caught-and-bowled Cummins took to dismiss opener Abdulla Shafique who'd made 62.

But Babar, a former Pakistan captain and it's best batsman in all forms, and among the best batsmen in the world, wouldn't have been too worried.

Pat Cummins was keen to get at Babar again, having already worked him over in the Perth Test.

Babar facing, with a single to his name, saw the ball leave Cummins' right hand. He moved forward slightly to play a defensive stroke at where it was going to pitch. The ball wobbled noticeably in the air, but that didn't faze Babar – he would have felt he had it covered.

But he didn't get bat on ball. He certainly heard the roar of the big crowd and he surely heard the sound above the tumult of his stumps being reorganised.

He turned to see the damage before advancing to check where the ball had pitched. He was bemused.

There was no need for a replay or a review. Babar was on his way. He looked at his batting partner who could only offer a shrug of the shoulders.

Babar watched the replay on the big screen as he walked off. The ball had missed the inside edge of his bat and clipped the bail on the off-stump. How did it deviate so much?

Until that moment, Babar had enjoyed success against Cummins. He'd faced balls from him more than 200 times in Test Cricket, scoring 122 runs. His was a prized wicket for Australia, with recent Test scores to his name of 104, 97, 36, 196, 67 and 55.

Cummins had come up with something special. Maybe not in the class of Shane Warne's "ball of the century" that successfully spun around Mike Gatting on 4 June 1993 and clattered into the stumps on the second day of the first Test of the 1993 Ashes series, at Old Trafford in Manchester. It was Warne's first ball against England, in his first Ashes Test and a ball that brought leg-spin bowling back into popularity.

How did you do that? was the question asked of Cummins.

"It's a dream ball. It's what you try most balls, but it's rare that it comes off," he said. "That wasn't a deliberate ball to seam in. That's 50-50 that it's going to seam in or out. Try and create a bit of an angle and if

I don't know what it's doing, hopefully the batter doesn't know either." Babar certainly didn't know.

It was a bit of MCG magic and it certainly got the crowd crowing.

In days past that would have earned Cummins massive chants each time he ran in afterwards. The crowd was well pleased but perhaps the name Cummins doesn't lend itself to the chants that had accompanied other bowlers on their long run in.

An MCG crowd usually is lively. Chants used to ring out all day. Lil-lee, Lil-lee, Lil-lee and later, War-nee, War-nee, War-nee were designed to inspire the Australians to victory.

Cummins was at the centre of controversy in Australia's second innings, when given out caught by keeper Rizwan. Cummins looked bemused, not believing he'd hit the ball. He called for a review and that's where things went weird.

The DRS showed no mark on Hotspot where the bat might have touched the ball and replays showed clean air. But a faint spike appeared on Snicko and the umpire stuck to his original decision.

Maybe this hot-shot technology was not the panacea everyone thought.

• • •

Australia has done well at the MCG, but not consistently until the past decade. Of 112 Tests since 1877, the home side has won 63, lost 31 and drawn 18, and usually has been hard to beat.

Allan Border has played the most Tests there, 20. Greg Chappell, Rod Marsh and Steve Waugh have played 17. Several played Tests there 11 times, including The Don (Bradman) and Shane Warne.

Australia three times has scored 600+ totals, the best 8d-624 against Pakistan in December 2016. David Warner, Steve Smith and Azhar Ali all scored centuries. Australia won by an innings and 18 runs.

The highest individual score there has been Australian Bob Cowper's 589-ball 307 in 12 hours at the crease in 1966.

The best bowling there was by Australian Arthur Mailey's 9-121 in England's second innings of the fourth Test of the 1920-21 Ashes series.

It is also the best bowling performance in an innings by an Australian.

Mailey bowled leg-breaks and googlies.

Around 70 years later, another leg-break exponent was the hero of the G, Shane Warne, of course.

Warne played his first Test at the MCG on Boxing Day, 1992, against the West Indies. His return on a wearing pitch on the fifth day was 7-52. It was only his fifth Test match.

In 1994, Warne took a hat-trick in the Boxing Day Ashes Test, the first hat-trick there in 90 years – since Hugh Trumble in 1904. (Trumble also took a hat-trick at the MCG in 1902).

Warne took his 700th Test wicket against the old enemy – England – on the first day of the fourth Ashes Test at the MCG in 2006. It was Warne's last Test and he took a wicket with his last ball in a five-wicket haul for the match.

Opposition bowlers used to cop plenty of sledging for boisterous crowds still under the effects of Christmas spirit (or some other tipple). The names of Hadlee, Wasim etc were called out followed by "is a wanker". The players usually took it in good spirits, even in the case of Wasim Akram when he thought the cheers were FOR him until the batter up the other end, his captain Imran Khan, revealed to him what the "w" word meant. Wasim took it well and the chants actually died down when he acknowledged Bay 13.

The noise rarely abated, even in the dying stages of the day's play when some fans a little tired and emotional were being escorted from the ground by people in uniform to chants of "you're going home in a divvy van".

Heaven forbid if the game became boring later in the match. The crowd would then resort to the Mexican wave to entertain themselves and boo those (usually in the Members) who failed to take part. Or a beach ball would appear from somewhere and be passed among the throng until it intruded on the field to be confiscated by a security person.

There was nothing better than watching Australia get off to "flyer" against the old enemy on Boxing Day at the G.

There have been some magnificent bowling feats there.

Dennis Lillee had his moment in the sun, too, getting West Indies superstar Viv Richards out with the last ball of the opening day of the 1981 Boxing Day Test.

A year later, Allan Border and Jeff Thomson came within a whisker of pulling off what would have been a remarkable victory in the fourth Test of the Ashes series. The two made a last-wicket stand requiring 37 runs when they started but came up three runs short.

In the modern era, the name Pat Cummins appears on the list four times in the past decade for taking five wickets in an innings. Two of those came in the one Test, against Pakistan in 2023. He also claimed five in the 2018 loss to India and in the 2019 victory over New Zealand.

Cummins has an impressive record at the G. He has played seven Tests and taken 35 wickets at 17.0 and has the best record of those who have played more than four Tests and taken more than 10 wickets.

Other Australians who boast a five-for in recent times include rising Test star Cameron Green against South Africa in 2022.

And of course, one of the most memorable day's cricket at the G was against the Old Enemy in December 2021 when Scot Boland, until then unheralded and unheard of in Test cricket, intervened to dash any hope England might have held for winning back The Ashes.

By the time the Ashes series reached Melbourne in 2021 Australia led 2-0 and victory would mean the Ashes stayed in Australia's possession.

Enter Scott Boland, the second indigenous Australian to play Test cricket, following in the footsteps of Jason Gillespie several years before.

Boland had been Sheffield Shield Player of the Year in 2019, but with Cummins, Starc and Hazlewood ahead of him in the fast-bowling pecking order his name was seldom mentioned as a Test cricket prospect, and indeed almost certainly he would not have played in the Boxing Day Test of 2021 had Hazlewood been available.

Boland intervened to wrap up England's hope of winning back the Ashes in no uncertain terms. England began the match down 2-0 with three to play. Boland effectively made sure England weren't going to be packing The Urn in the hand-luggage.

Nothing like his 6-7 in four devastating overs (and five wickets in 19 balls) had ever been seen in Test Cricket on Australian soil, let alone at the G.

To some close watchers of cricket, Boland was regarded as an MCG specialist, his Boxing Day Test haul taking him to 101 wickets there. He went on the return Ashes tour to England but has since plied his trade in domestic cricket and some County cricket in the UK.

It will be a long time before his MCG performance in 2021 will be forgotten.

Since Bay 13 was consumed by the Great Southern Stand in the great MCG revamp of 1990, the chanting doesn't quite have the same ring to it. It works better when "ee" is at the end of it. But it "ain't what it used to be" anymore.

Fans were not impressed by the removal of Bay 13, by the way. Many bemoaned that it had become "yuppified" with the installation of new $195-a-head seating. The upside has been a decline in ugly crowd behaviour and families attending the cricket are probably grateful for that, particularly when the cost of a ticket is so expensive.

Some of the great moments at the cricket will be remembered for a long time. The Barmy Army travelling with England always brought humour to the ground, as did the Richies, Australian fans' tribute to the great Richie Benaud, resplendent in their ties, silver-haired wigs and beige jackets.

The sight of Merv Hughes warming up near the boundary always got the crowd behind up and about, joining in unison.

Current Test batsman Travis Head paid tributed to long retired-Merv's routine to great applause during the Boxing Day Test of 2023 against Pakistan.

The MCG has been the scene of some amazing batting moments, too. One that is often recalled is the appearance back at the wicket of Australian Rick McCosker with his head heavily bandaged after copping a jaw-breaking blow from Bob Willis during the Centenary Test in 1977. Even 40+ years later people would still ask him "how's the jaw."

The MCG also holds the record for a single-day Test record crowd, 90,800 in 1961 when Australia played the West Indies.

The G also has been the scene of some unsavoury incidents. Racist taunts, streakers, fights and abuse were all dealt with severely as officials sought to keep cricket family-friendly.

The Sydney Cricket ground is iconic in its own way, famous for the Hill and the ground where Don Bradman set out on what is still the most notable Test batting career, finishing with an unmatched average of 99.9.

FOOTNOTE: The Melbourne Cricket Ground is the largest stadium in the Southern Hemisphere, the 11th largest in the world and the second-largest cricket ground by capacity, after the Narendra Modi Stadium in India. It was built in 1853 when the club was forced to move from its South Melbourne site because of the establishment of Victoria's steam railway from Melbourne to Sandridge (Port Melbourne).

The ground was the centrepiece of the 1956 Olympic Games and has hosted VFL/AFL grand finals for many years, the T20 World Cup final in 2022, Women's T20 World Cup, international Rugby Union matches, State of Origin Rugby League matches, 2000 Olympic Games soccer and World Cup qualifying matches and a range of concerts.

A Billy Graham evangelistic crusade in 1959 attracted more than 140,000 people, mostly standing. The MCG hosted both the first Test match and the first One Day International, played between Australia and England in 1877 and 1971, respectively.

The MCG was redeveloped in time for the 2006 Commonwealth Games, with the completion of the new Ponsford, Members and Olympic Stands and again upgraded in 2012. The MCG's capacity remains at 100,000, including seating for 95,000 spectators.

In 2022, plans were announced for a possible $1 billion redevelopment.

8

MORE BANG FOR THE BUCK

Who would want to be a bowler in the Indian Premier League?

The 17th season of the big-money Indian T20 competition was a batter's bonanza. Bowlers took a caning in the slugfest as several thousand times they watched deliveries belted into the stands or crash into the boundary ropes.

By the end of the 2024 final, won by Kolkata Knight Riders, 1,260 sixes had been hit off the hapless bowlers, the most sixes in IPL history. Batters are the heroes.

Yet the two players who sold for the highest prices at the pre-season auction were fast bowlers – Australian Test stars Mitchell Starc and Pat Cummins.

They are among the top-ranked bowlers in the world in the longer form of the game, but why would they subject themselves to such torture as they would face in the IPL?

Maybe it is the money. Maybe it is the challenge. Maybe it is the desire for experience on the sub-continent. It may be a good way for bowlers to hone their skills in short-form cricket. It may even be put down to a lack of cricket for the Australians for a large part of the year.

Cummins was appointed captain of the team that paid big money for his services. The leadership experience in T20 probably would be good for him. It turned out to be good for Sunrisers Hyderabad (SRH), finishing second on the 2024 ladder by winning eight of their 14 games to go into the finals in May.

SRH encountered Kolkata Knight Riders (KKR) twice in the playoffs, including the final but suffered big defeats both times. Such was the capitulation in the final on 26 May that Cummins was top-scorer for SRH with 24 as KKR won by eight wickets. A Travis Head duck to start the SRH innings didn't bode well, and the side was all out in just under 11 overs. Cummins took one of the only two KKR wickets to fall.

Bragging rights went to Cummins' fellow Australian strike bowler (and auction record-holder) Mitchell Starc of KKR, named man-of-the-match for his 2-14 from three overs.

Nevertheless, 2024 was SRH's best year in the IPL for four years.

Before the season started, there was some disappointment that Cummins had replaced South African Aiden Markram as captain. One unhappy pundit was former South African cricketer AB de Villiers, who expressed surprise and disappointment.

According to *crictoday.com*, de Villiers was concerned about the possible influence of Australian connections within the SRH franchise. He cited the appointment of Cummins, the presence of Vettori (coach of both SRH and assistant to the Australian national team) as suggesting an "Australian flavour" was taking over the team.

Another who voiced concern was Indian spinner Ravi Ashwin. "Sunrisers have won two titles in SA20 (South African Sunrisers' franchise), and Markram was their captain. I was shocked when he was removed from the captaincy of SRH in IPL," Ashwin said.

Cummins did have one notable former player in his corner, one of the game's greatest opening batters and former Indian captain, Sunil Gavaskar.

"I believe getting Pat Cummins was a good move, although it might have been a bit pricey," Gavaskar said. "He'll add leadership to their team, which they were missing before. Last season, some of the bowling decisions in important games were confusing and led to losses. With

Pat Cummins as captain now, I'm confident it'll improve the team's performance."

Gavaskar makes an interesting point about the role of bowlers in a T20 match. The short-form game requires a bowler to think about every delivery as one that could take a wicket. In the longer forms of the game, a bowler has time to set up the batter for a possible wicket, something in which Pat Cummins had expertise.

In any event, the critics were silenced when Cummins took the Sunrisers into the 2024 IPL final against KKR.

Sunrisers finished last in the league in 2023. With Cummins at the helm and fellow Aussie Travis Head in sublime form (until two failures in the play-off games), a year later SRH was contending for the title.

Cummins had not played a T20I match for almost 15 months before representing Australia in two T20Is against New Zealand in February 2024.

Head and Abhishek Sharma became one of the most lethal combination of openers in the IPL. And the team set a record for the highest IPL total, twice.

Starc was one of the bowlers who copped quite a bit of stick in the preliminary rounds.

In his first eight games, he took just seven wickets with an economy of 11.78 and conceded more than 50 three times.

But as the competition ambled towards the play-offs, he seemed to find some form that included 4-33 against the Mumbai Indians, before hitting his straps in the finals, taking 5-48 in the two play-off matches against SRH. He finished the season with 17 wickets in 14 matches.

Cummins pulled off a rare thing in IPL cricket in a match against the Mumbai Indians in May 2024. He bowled 12 dot-balls that included a wicket-maiden. But that effort and the two top scores, by him and Travis Head, were not enough to get a win.

The captaincy nous of Cummins and his ability with the ball and bat were both on show in the IPL, the latter giving Australia something to look forward to in the T20I World Cup. Cummins was not captain for the World Cup but his bowling experience from the IPL would be invaluable.

The IPL is arranged in two groups and each of the 10 teams play fourteen games before the play-off series.

SRH no doubt had been impressed by Cummins' record as captain of Australian teams in Tests and ODIs when they nominated him as leader. As well, he had played in a winning IPL team.

He first played in the IPL in 2014 for KKR who were IPL premiers that year. He played again in the annual tournament in 2015, 2017 (Delhi Capitals) and 2020-21-22 (back to KKR) before going to Sunrisers Hyderabad (SRH) in 2024.

The A$3.1m KKR paid for him in 2021 was a record for the IPL at that time. In the 2022 market, however, the franchise cut his pay packet by more than half, to A$1.343m. He played only five games in 2022, before returning home with a hip injury. He didn't play in 2023.

In the IPL auction for the 2014 season, he was for about two hours the most expensive player in IPL history again (A$3.67 million – 20.5 crore rupees), surpassed by Australian teammate and fellow fast bowler Mitchell Starc, bought by KKR for A$4.42 million (24.75 crore rupees) after a bidding war with the Gujarat Titans. Starc had been missing from the IPL since 2015.

One who questioned whether Cummins was worth that kind of money in T20 cricket was former Australian fast bowler and appointed coach of Sri Lanka in 2024, Jason Gillespie.

Gilliespie said on SEN radio: "Pat's obviously a quality bowler and a quality leader, we've seen that…I just don't think T20 is his best format. I think he's a Test bowler, personally. I think Test cricket is his absolute bread and butter.

"He's a good T20 bowler, make no mistake – but that's massive overs for me."

To be fair, Gillespie no doubt was talking about Cummins the bowler, before he was appointed captain. The value of captaincy was somewhat indeterminable, but of considerable value to SRH, and justified by the team's rise from last place in 2023 to top-four a year later.

Also to be fair, Cummins' bowling record in 2024 wasn't bad. He claimed 18 wickets from 16 matches at an average of 31.44. He'd been useful with the bat, too – 136 runs at an average of 22.67 and a highest score of 35 not out.

The previous highest IPL contract was held by England all-rounder Sam Curran, signed by the Punjab Kings for A$3.3 million (18.5 crore rupees) in 2023.

Cummins also held one other IPL record, albeit also briefly, in 2022 when he scored the fastest 50 in the IPL, from 14 balls when playing for KKR against Mumbai Indians. The record was broken by Rajasthan Royals' Yashasvi Jaiswal in 2023, by one ball.

On the eve of his first match as captain of SRH in 2024 Cummins said leading an IPL team had its challenges.

"You play 14 games in six-seven weeks, plus finals. I'm used to playing a lot of Test cricket, so four overs isn't as taxing on your body. But it can be mentally taxing, the travel, obviously a different country, play a new team every few days you have to prepare for…

"But it's nothing new, we've done it before. Obviously, the game day is most important…you have expectations, you have a lot of fans who demand a lot out of the team, they want results. Yeah, being captain is probably a little bit more responsibility. But it's not much different to what we're used to as players. We'll give it our best."

Their best was impressive.

SRH set a record on 8 May 2024 (Pat Cummins' 31st birthday) when they restricted Lucknow Super Giants to 4-165 and chased down the total in less than 10 overs and without losing a wicket, thanks to Travis Head's 89 off 30 balls and Abhishek Sharma's 75 off 28. The openers hit 16 fours and 14 sixes. Pat's father, Peter was there to help his son celebrate his birthday.

It was the biggest margin for a completing a run chase of 150 or more in IPL history and the 167 total was the highest score by any team by the end of the tenth over in men's T20 history.

The Hyderabad crowd warmed to their captain. They sang "Happy Birthday" to him before the match with the Super Giants.

Cummins was asked by the Indian press how he was finding captaincy in the IPL.

"The biggest difference is that you know your team-mates really well playing for Australia. There's a lot of things that don't need to be said, because I have played with Joshie Hazlewood and Starc for 15 years. So there's a real kind of trust and you just don't really need to say much, everything kind of runs by itself," Cummins said.

"I think here, learning some new players, that's…the biggest difference, and just learning those different roles within the team. I know a few of the other guys, obviously, and have done a bit of homework to try and get the best out of the guys. But that's probably going to be the biggest difference."

How different was captaincy in T20s from Tests and ODIs?

"Very different," he said. "Test cricket is a bit more gradual. In T20 cricket it can all happen in five minutes. It can be a big over and suddenly the game's changed. So, every ball, you've got to think on your feet. You've got to be really clear on what you want to achieve with that ball or it can get away from you quickly."

Cummins reached two bowling milestones in the 2024 season, 50 IPL wickets and 150 wickets in all T20 matches. Three other Australians had taken more than 50 wickets in the IPL – Shane Watson (92), Mitchell Johnson (61) and Shane Warne (57).

• • •

Cummins was praised for an example of sportsmanship in an IPL match between SRH and Chennai Super Kings (CSK) at the Rajiv Gandhi International Cricket Stadium in Hyderabad in April 2024.

Sportsmanship or a clever tactical ploy?

SRH appealed for obstructing the field against batter Ravindra

Jadeja, well-known to the Australians from recent Test series.

The third umpire most likely would have given Jadeja out after he ran between the ball and the stumps. He changed direction and the ball hit him instead of the stumps. The incident happened in the 19th over.

What happened next seemed to be an act of generosity. Cummins withdrew the appeal and Jadeja continued, remaining unbeaten on 31 runs off 23 balls as CSK posted 5-165 in 20 overs.

SRH went on to win the match with six wickets in hand and 11 balls to spare.

All seemed hunky-dory. But a question was asked: did Cummins withdraw the appeal to keep Jadeja at the wicket? That was considered a possibility as the next man in was to be one of the greatest exponents in India of T20 batting, MS Dhoni. He would have been capable of some damaging batting to get quick runs.

Withdrawing the appeal may have been an astute piece of captaincy.

The 17th edition of the IPL began in March 2024, 10 teams taking part. It ended with the play-offs in the last week of May.

Cummins was the third Australian to captain SRH, after Cameron White and David Warner. New Zealander Kane Williamson also is a former captain.

For all the high-profile captains and players, SRH had only won the IPL trophy once, when led by David Warner in 2016.

• • •

In April 2024, Cummins figured in two noteworthy incidents in a match against the Punjab Kings, involving two players from the "old enemy."

Jonny Bairstow, probably still not overly comfortable facing Australians after the runout incident from the Ashes series a few months previously, was on strike to Cummins.

Cummins steamed in for the first over of Kings' innings. Bairstow survived two balls before trying to hit the third to the leg side, creating only a breeze as the ball clattered untouched into his stumps, out for 0.

Cummins was again prominent in the field a few overs later in the dismissal of another Englishman, Sam Curran.

Curran mistimed a pull shot, the ball flying over long off and looking likely to evade Cummins. But the skipper scrambled backwards with a leap into the air that saw him grab the ball before he tumbled to the ground.

Sunrisers managed a modest total of 9-182 and the Kings fell two runs short in the final over (6-180).

The two efforts by Cummins during the Punjab Kings innings were critical, justification for the "big bucks."

• • •

Recruiting Travis Head proved a master stroke for SRH.

Coming off his match-sealing century in the ODI World Cup final, he carried his form into the IPL, no doubt to the extreme pleasure of his captain, again.

Head blasted his second T20 century (his first in the IPL) with 102 runs off 41 balls against RCB, helping Sunrisers Hyderabad to a record score in a victory over Royal Challengers Bengaluru (RCB) in April. SRH's score of 3-287 was the highest in IPL history. Cummins took three wickets despite going for 10 runs an over in RCB's innings.

Head cost the Sunrisers 6.80 crore rupees (A$1.22 million). He scored 296 runs, fourth highest for the season (Virat Kohli led with 741 runs).

Young Sunrisers batter Abhishek Sharma emerged as one of the best India hopefuls in the short game. He put a lot of his success down to the dressing room environment.

"It was a pretty easy message from all the coaches and our captain (Pat Cummins), I would say. They were pretty clear with all the batters, just go out and express yourself," Sharma said.

"I think that's really simple and a powerful message coming from the coach or the captain, because if you see as a youngster or as a batter, a top-order batter, you just have to get that confidence from your captain and coach. I think we got that from day one and it's our job to just go there and just play our game."

Sharma also praised his opening partner, Travis Head.

"Batting with Travis it's obviously joyful to watch him always. We've been talking a lot off the field, so I think that's helping. Obviously he's someone I'm looking forward to bat with," the 23-year-old said.

Sunrisers head coach was New Zealander Daniel Vettori, also an assistant coach of the Australian national team.

PAT CUMMINS IPL 2024: 16 matches; 61 overs, 18 wickets, 566 runs, Av 31.44, econ 9.28, best 3-43.

Batting: 136 runs, Av 22.67.

• • •

The basic rules in the IPL are the same as for T20Is, but in the IPL, substitutes (the "impact player" rule) are permitted during a game.

Substitutions can be made either before the start of an innings; at the end of the over; at the fall of a wicket; or when a batter retires. Once replaced, the substituted player can take no further part in the match, not even field.

The substitute can replace any player from the starting XI at any point before the end of the 14th over of either innings and is allowed to bat and bowl his full quota of overs.

There is also a rule about slow-over rates, the penalty being fielding restrictions.

The 10 IPL sides play 14 group games each – seven at home and seven away – with the top four then progressing to the play-offs.

PAT CUMMINS

AUSTRALIANS IN THE IPL 2024

Delhi Capitals: Mitch Marsh (A$1.2m), David Warner (A$1.16m), Jhye Richardson (A$890,000), Jake Fraser-McGurk (A$92,000)

Gujarat Titans: Spencer Johnson (A$1.78m), Matthew Wade (A$446,000)

Kolkata Knight Riders: Mitchell Starc (A$4.43m)

Lucknow Super Giants: Marcus Stoinis (A$1.7m), Ashton Turner (A$178,000)

Mumbai Indians: Tim David (A$1.53m)

Punjab Kings: Nathan Ellis (A$135,000)

Royal Challengers Bangalore: Cameron Green (A$3.15m), Glenn Maxwell (A$2m)

Sunrisers Hyderabad: Pat Cummins (A$3.67m), Travis Head (A$1.2m).

Fraser-McGurk replaced Warner in the squad mid-way through the season.

They were all possible inclusions in an Australian T20 line-up.

• • •

Former Australian captain Ricky Ponting identified McGurk as the "next Warner who could play for Australia in all three formats of the game."

Eyebrows were raised when he wasn't initially selected in Australia's squad for the 2024 T20I World Cup, but he and Matt Short later were added as "travelling reserves" to cover for possible fitness issues with Warner and captain Mitch Marsh.

It is worth looking at Fraser-McGurk's IPL season with the Delhi Capitals, even though the team didn't make it to the play-offs.

MORE BANG FOR THE BUCK

He scored 330 runs across nine games, averaging 36.66. He made four half-centuries, three of which were from 19 balls or fewer. His strike-rate was 234.04. No other batter with at least 300 IPL runs had a better strike rate. Next best was Travis Head (179.13).

Fraser-McGurk was the bargain buy of the season.

• • •

Where does all the money in the IPL come from?

The Forbes financial publication in 2009, the second year of the IPL, put the average value of the league's eight franchises at US$67 million (A$100 million).

When the IPL expanded to 10 franchises that figure more likely came close to US$1.04 billion.

Around 80% of the IPL's revenue in a typical year comes from revenue negotiated by the Board of Control for Cricket in India (BCCI). The pot includes the media rights agreement with Star India and sponsorships that were in 2021 worth US$58 million.

Other revenue comes from ticket sales, merchandise and investment in franchises.

More than 20 countries conduct T20 cricket leagues, not all are franchise-based, however.

The major franchise leagues are IPL (the first in 2008-09), the Pakistan Super League (PSL), Australia's Big Bash, the T20 Blast conducted by the ECB in the UK, the Bangladesh Premier League and the Caribbean Premier League. Recent additions to T20 leagues include the UAE, which also hosts a Masters series for retired cricketers, Sri Lanka, Afghanistan and the US.

Major League Cricket was established in the US in 2023 with six teams. Two of the teams were backed by Cricket Victoria and Cricket NSW from Australia.

MLC is operated by American Cricket Enterprises (ACE) and sanctioned by USA Cricket. Minor League Cricket (MiLC), a youth league, also started in 2023, contested by 27 franchise-based teams.

PAT CUMMINS

Players who took part in the inaugural US season included Faf du Plessis (South Africa), Marcus Stoinis, Aaron Finch (both Australia) Trent Boult (New Zealand), Quinton de Kock (South Africa) and Jason Roy (England).

The 2024 competition was scheduled to start just a couple of weeks after the T20 world Cup in the West Indies and the US, the aim being to capitalise on interest generated by the world's best short-form cricketers. Several top players stayed on after the World Cup to play in the MLC.

Australians playing for the six teams in the 2024 MLC included Adam Zampa, Spencer Johnson, Alex Carey, Tim David, Pat Cummins, Josh Inglis, Matt Short, Jake Fraser-McGurk, Brody Couch (domestic signing), Nathan Ellis, Lance Morris, Cameron Gannon (domestic signing), Aaron Hardie, Cameron Stevenson (domestic signing), Glenn Maxwell, Travis Head, Steve Smith, Jack Edwards, Andrew Tye, Ian Holland (domestic signing).

Players from South Africa, England and Pakistan were among other nations represented.

Ricky Ponting was coaching the Washington Freedom. Other teams were LA Knight Riders, MI New York, San Franciso Unicorns, Seattle Orcas and Texas Super Kings.

Three MLC teams are owned by IPL franchises; Texas Super Kings (Chennai Super Kings), Los Angeles Knight Riders (Kolkata Knight Riders) and MI New York (Mumbai Indians).

Indian superstars are not allowed to play in any T20 franchise leagues outside the IPL. Australian players are allowed to hop on the T20 merry-go-round as long as it does not clash with their international commitments.

Just as Australia began its T20 World Cup campaign, it was revealed Pat Cummins had signed a four-year deal with the Unicorns in the US.

Cummins justified the interest in him as a marquee signing in the American league with back-to-back hat-tricks in the World Cup in June, against Bangladesh and in a loss to Afghanistan. He could have had four in a row (a double hat-trick) in the Afghanistan game if David Warner had held on to a relatively simple catch.

The MLC was given official List A status as it began its second season; performances could be included in official statistics.

Cummins said: "MLC is developing at a rapid rate, and the US market potential is huge for cricket.

"While cricket is integral to my involvement, the global network and long-term possibilities offered by the owners specifically, and Silicon Valley more broadly, presented a unique opportunity for me and my life beyond cricket."

The Unicorns are co-owned by Silicon Valley entrepreneurs Anand Rajaraman and Venky Harinarayan.

MLC investors also included three Indian IPL franchises, Microsoft CEO Satya Nadella and Ross Perot Jr. MLC plans to build stadiums and first-class facilities to accelerate cricket's development in the US.

9

A COURAGEOUS DECISION

Failure will never overtake me if my determination to succeed is strong enough.

PAT CUMMINS

Cricket fans had only limited access to the thoughts of Pat Cummins as he took over the captaincy of the Australian Test team – the appointment on 26 November 2021 came in the midst of Covid-19 lockdowns.

Such an announcement usually would be met with great fanfare and a massive press conference in which the news-gatherers would be hanging on every word, throwing questions from all directions. Not in lockdown.

The obvious question: How could he juggle his responsibilities as skipper with those of being the team's premier fast bowler?

When Australia toured England in 2019, Cummins claimed 29 wickets for 211 runs – no pace bowler sent down more overs or took more wickets.

He was still going to be the key player in Australia's attack in England's return visit in 2021-22.

The scrutiny he faced as he led Australian into his first series as captain, the Ashes at stake, was going to be immense. There could be no bigger test of his mettle.

A COURAGEOUS DECISION

Former England captain Mike Brearley argued in his book *Art of Captaincy* that only "as a last resort" should fast bowlers be appointed as captain.

"It takes an exceptional character to know when to bowl, to keep bowling with all his energy screwed up into a ball of aggression, and to be sensitive to the needs of the team, tactically and psychologically," Brearley said.

Cummins probably never read the book. He was – and is – an exceptional character. He was by no means "a last resort."

Brearley was a noted captain; he had a modest Test batting record (average 22.88 from 39 Tests) and didn't bowl in a Test match. Joe Root averaged 47.7 while he was the England captain in 59 Tests for 27 wins (and he bowled a bit).

The perception was Brearley was in the team as captain because of his leadership qualities. His record as captain wasn't bad – 31 Tests for 18 victories and only 4 losses between 1977 and 1981.

Cummins began his Test captaincy in remarkable style, with eight wins from 13 games, including a series win in Pakistan.

How would Cummins rate as captain compared to the "greats" from eras past?

Steve Waugh was captain for 57 Tests, victorious in 44 and losing only 9. Ricky Ponting was captain in 77 Tests, winning 48 and losing just 16.

At times, Cummins faced criticism as being a defensive captain yet that hasn't defined his captaincy and the team's record tells a different story – to repeat, two international trophies won, and the Ashes retained.

A look at the record of two immediate past captains, Steve Smith and Tim Paine, shows that at the end of 2023, Cummins was holding his own.

He had a 52.4 winning percentage (wins from matches captained), with draws and losses both at 23.8%, from 21 Tests.

Tim Paine had a 47.8 winning percentage, 34.8% losses and 17.4%

draws, from 23 matches in charge. He lost his first four matches in charge.

Steve Smith had a winning percentage of 55.3, losses 26.3% and draws 18.4% from 38 matches.

According to *Howstat* figures, the least successful Australian captain was Kim Hughes. His teams won only four Tests of the 28 in which he was captain. To be fair, Australia wasn't doing so well in his tenure which coincided with the presence of the breakaway World Series Cricket where many from Australia's Test team at the time had gone.

Had captaincy had any effect on Cummins' individual performance?

That's hard to say but two figures are worth mentioning: his bowling average as captain was 25.89, compared to 21.59 previously.

Not too much should be read into that as he has used himself in attack a little differently to previous captains. For one thing, he has become something of a game-changer, able to turn Tests around in quick time.

A case in point: The Boxing Day Test against Pakistan in 2023 where in just four balls he claimed two wickets.

With the visitors 1-105 and looking like making a serious challenge, Cummins put himself back in the attack.

Immediately, he slowed the scoring rate that had been better than 4.5 an over.

He conceded only two singles and a two in the first 17 balls of his new spell. The rest were dot-balls.

He took the wickets of Abdullah Shafique (62) and Babar Azam (1) to spark a first innings collapse of 5-46. His caught-and-bowled of Shafique was inspirational stuff, with athleticism not always seen from a fast bowler who had just sent down a 140 km/h rocket.

The ball that bowled Azam was something else, a "dream ball."

Captaincy in deciding when to bowl himself may have played a part, but his 5-48 and 5-49 in that Test showed he was still very much a match-winner, as well as a leader.

A COURAGEOUS DECISION

That's not to say he hasn't had bad days.

The Thursday of the fourth Old Trafford Test in July 2023 was one.

Australia batted first, sent in and, frankly, struggled. Had rain not intervened it could have been a debacle.

England rolled Australia for 317, quite a bit short of an innings that would be competitive. Things didn't go well for the captain; he drove the first ball he faced from James Anderson to Ben Stokes, out for 1.

Bazball was evident when England batted. Led by 189 from Zac Crawly the home side's batters blasted their way to 592. Probably the only upside was that Bairstow didn't make 100, left not out on 99.

Cumins took some stick, his sole wicket (that of his opposing captain Stokes for 56) came at a cost of 129 from 23 overs. Fellow quick Josh Hazlewood didn't fare a lot better, conceding 126 runs from 27 overs, but claiming two wickets. Australia was 5-214 in reply when play ended, ironically England's winning chance killed off by English weather.

Cummins also had a horrid time in the field, twice missing the chance to catch Moeen Ali who made 54 and figured in early productive partnerships.

A backing-up mistake also saw a throw from Steve Smith escape Cummins, and he copped plenty from the English fans as he chased it down towards the boundary.

Even an Ashes-winning captain can have a bad day.

Ian Chappell enjoys legendary status in Australian cricket. He captained Australian teams between 1971 and 1975 and more recently has lent his expertise to commentary.

At the end of 2023 he expressed a simple thought about Pat Cummins' Test captaincy: "Any cricketer who isn't inspired by Cummins is in the wrong game."

He said there was no doubt Cummins ran the Australian team, not coach Andrew McDonald.

Chappell was one who didn't have many doubts that a fast bowler could lead the team. "I thought he'd be a good captain, but he has exceeded my expectations," Chappell said.

Cummins, Chappell said, was putting himself in the same category as Imran Khan of Pakistan, Richie Benaud of Australia and Ray Illingworth of England as the greatest bowling captains of all time.

Appointing Cummins as captain in 2021 was widely seen as a courageous move.

He was, after all, Australia's premier fast bowler who'd have plenty on his mind in whatever match he played without the extra responsibility of marshalling the troops.

Was he ready for that?

His leadership qualities were largely unknown and untested as far as many observers were concerned. His captaincy experience at a senior level was just four Marsh One-Day Cup games with NSW earlier in 2021.

But the inner sanctum of cricket administration had noticed something about the personable qualities of the young Sydneysider. They well knew his bowling capabilities.

Maybe future leadership was on their minds when they nominated him as a vice-captain in 2019 for the tour to Sri Lanka.

He celebrated his first match in the role with a 10-wicket haul. Bowling was still his forte.

Some commentators labelled him the accidental captain. That was quite a way from the truth, even though his ascendency to the top job was not something he or cricket administrators had planned to happen quite so soon.

Award-winning sports journalist Ron Reed described the Cummins rise in *Captain Pat: Cometh the Hour, Cummins the Man*, "Patrick James Cummins for most of his relatively young life, most notably from the day – November 17, 2011 – when he achieved the dream of countless thousands of young Australian men (and, these days, quite a few women as well) and became a Test cricketer, the 423rd man to wear the baggy green cap that distinguishes this proud and privileged cohort from every other exponent of the nation's most popular and important international sport.

A COURAGEOUS DECISION

"And he was just a boy of 18 years and 193 days, the second youngest ever to wear the iconic headwear behind Ian Craig, the precocious Sydney batsman who debuted, also against South Africa, in Melbourne in 1953, aged 17 and 239 days.

"Ten years later, almost to the very day, 26 November 2021, now 28, Cummins was appointed Australia's 47th Test captain, another huge achievement that neither he nor anybody else associated with the noble old game was expecting to happen, not at that particular juncture anyway. In the not too distant future, perhaps – but not yet."

Speculation about the possibility of Cummins assuming the captaincy one day "grew legs" in 2019 on India's tour of Australia for four Tests and Australia's return visit to India for ODIs and T20 matches.

He was described by some as the "new golden boy" of Australian cricket.

Then 25, he turned on career-best performances with ball and bat in the Third Test against India with match figures of 9-99 and an impressive knock of 63 runs in Australia's second innings. India won the Test and retained the Border-Gavaskar Trophy.

Australia won both short-form series in India in the return tour. Cummins was the leading wicket-taker (14) in the 3-2 series win by Australia in the ODIs. He took 2-59 in the two-match T20 series won 2-0 by Australia.

He rose to Nos 3 and 7 on the ICC Test bowling and all-rounder rankings respectively, giving rise to speculation about captaincy, the theory being that the captain had to know something about batting and bowling.

Cummins described the talk as "nonsense".

He had been endorsed by Dennis Lillee and Steve Waugh as Australia's Test "captain-in-waiting".

Lillee, speaking to *cricket.com.au*, had no doubt Cummins was up to the job.

"He's an intelligent guy but more than that, he's got real cricket smarts," Lillee said in article coinciding with the 10th anniversary of Cummins' Test debut.

"He's a born leader. He's 110 per cent all the time, whether the wicket is flat or not, and I admire that in a fast bowler. He's a leader of men and they look up to him." Lillee knew a fair bit about fast bowling of course and he was to play a significant part in the ascendency of Cummins to the ranks of Test "greats".

But was the Cummins appointment just a stop-gap measure while Australian cricket sorted itself out in the aftermath of the 2018 controversy in South Africa? The episode cost Steve Smith the captaincy, then the sexting scandal of 2021 ultimately forced his replacement, Tim Paine, to abdicate.

Australian cricket had to find someone to lead them out of the public relations mire, and quickly. Administrators turned to Paine's vice-captain, Pat Cummins, who it was said had the character, charm and charisma that Australian cricket so desperately needed.

London's *Evening Standard* newspaper said: "Australian cricket just became that little bit more difficult to dislike." (The press might have wanted to retract that after the 2023 Ashes series).

Ron Reed again (2021): "It is hard to think of any Australian captain who has come to the post with so much goodwill. Long before this life-changing development, he had become – to employ a cliché that does not sit comfortably with his own self-estimation – the Golden Boy of the Australian game.

"There were multiple reasons for that. Not only was he a brilliant player in all three forms of the game – officially recognised as the world's best fast bowler for the past two years – but he was also highly intelligent, and, not to be underestimated, blessed with the good looks of a film star.

"Tall, dark and handsome seems an understatement. As a package, it was beyond pleasing – impossible to dislike, in fact. He had never been involved in any lurid behaviour or trouble-making, unless you wanted to count that he was a member of the team that was responsible

A COURAGEOUS DECISION

for the ball-tampering scandal...there was never any suggestion that Cummins, or the other fast bowlers, Mitchell Starc and Josh Hazlewood, were involved in illegally sandpapering the ball – cheating, in other words.

"Personality has always been regarded as a crucial component whenever the Cricket Australia directors have to decide on a new figurehead, every bit as important as playing ability. That's because they jealously protect the long-held public assertion that there is no more prestigious post in all of Australian sport, and very few in any area of public life. There has always been a sort of urban myth that it ranks only a single rung behind the Prime Ministership, which may or may not have been true in days gone by. Bradman, for instance, was more revered than any politician – but which is probably more romantic than rational these days.

"Nonetheless, when the day arrived to assess Cummins' suitability for the role, this concept mattered enormously. The previous two captains, Smith and Paine, had both departed in tears."

Steve Smith and teammates David Warner and Cameron Bancroft were banished from Australian representation for their roles in what became known as "sandpaper-gate". They were sent home. Smith and his deputy Warner were banned from international cricket for a year (leadership roles for at least two years) and Bancroft for nine months.

Paine didn't seem out of place in the captain's job. But he felt he should step aside "for the foreseeable future" when the texting incident became public.

Paine's resignation came just before Australia was due to take on old foe England on home soil in a battle for the Ashes.

Who was best man for the job?

Steve Smith was a possible candidate – he'd served his penance by then. He was said to be keen to get the captaincy back, having taken over from Michael Clarke in 2014 and winning 18 times, losing 10 and drawing six. But would the lingering fall-out from the South Africa episode rule him out?

PAT CUMMINS

Cummins had been vice-captain since 2019, appointed alongside Travis Head, and therefore considered to be a front-runner, particularly as Head lost the vice role towards the end of 2020, leaving Cummins as the sole deputy to Paine.

Ron Reed, himself a notable fast bowler at sub-representative level and who also captained teams, including one in which a visiting Ian Botham was a member, wrote: "Cummins was a specialist fast bowler, and no-one of that ilk had ever been entrusted with the Test captaincy, with the exception of Ray Lindwall who stepped in for one match in India in 1956 as a temporary replacement for the injured Ian Johnson.

"Yes, there are obviously reasons why on-field decision-making is more easily handled by batsmen who do not have the added mental strain of bowling themselves, but it has nevertheless always seemed to be an anachronism – not to mention an insult to some very good people who have specialised in that demanding skill for long periods.

"It hasn't stopped players from other countries, such as Pakistan's Imran Khan and Wasim Akram, England's Bob Willis, India's Kapil Dev, West Indies' Courtney Walsh and South Africa's Shaun Pollock, among others, making a reasonably successful fist of it."

Among the critical decisions a bowling captain would have to make was when to take the ball in hand himself. One luxury Cummins had was good knowledge of his bowling attack. Josh Hazlewood, Mitchell Starc and Nathan Lyon were all part of the NSW team, alongside Cummins. So, too, was vice-captain (and former captain) Steve Smith whose advice would be invaluable.

Obviously there would be questions about just how much influence Smith would have.

Cummins was the team's best bowler at that stage and his own efforts most likely would be pivotal in any Test.

The names of batters Cummins had dismissed the most demonstrates his importance as a bowler; Root (England) 11 times, Pujara (India) eight times; Buttler (England) seven times; Riswan (Pakistan) and Stokes (England) both six times.

A COURAGEOUS DECISION

His 10-wicket haul (5-18 in the second innings) in the Boxing Day Test against Pakistan at Melbourne's MCG in December 2023 further emphasised how he could be a match-winner from the bowling crease.

There was no question Australia needed such a performance from an express bowler. But could he be a good captain, too?

A notable player sceptical about a fast bowler leading a Test side was one of the world's best all-rounders in past years, Ian Botham (by now Sir), of England.

Ron Reed: "Botham was a close mate of Willis when he led England between 1982 and 1984. Sir Ian, who had a brief and unsuccessful crack at the captaincy himself as an all-rounder who bowled often enough to take 383 Test wickets, then a record for an Englishman, was sceptical about the chances of Cummins or any other fast bowler succeeding.

"Shortly after arriving in Australia to do TV commentary on the (2021-22) series, he said: 'You've got a new captain coming in. I wish him all the very best but it's going to be a difficult baptism. A fast bowler historically doesn't really work. I mean, when my great friend Bobby Willis, when he was captain, we virtually set the fields for him between balls because he was so focused running in quick and getting everything right at his end. The captaincy becomes, if anything, secondary in a bowler's thinking and planning'."

Nevertheless, Cummins took the reins. It was reported that he was asked to share any secrets (skeletons in the closet in other words) he might have had before he was given the job. It would have been a great relief that he was a "clean-skin."

The obvious next question (more by fans than officials) was how would he cope with being captain and a strike bowler.

"One of the big reasons why there's been talk around fast bowlers not being able to captain in the past is just the workload issue," Cummins told News Limited at the time.

"There are going to be times when I'm out in the middle, it's a hot day, I'm in the middle of a spell and I need to turn to people for advice, for tactics and for experience.

"How that looks? I think it potentially could look differently to what you've seen partnerships work like in the past.

"There will be times on the field where I'll throw to Steve (reinstated in a leadership role only as far as being vice-captain) and you'll see Steve move fielders around, maybe do bowling changes and take a bit more of an elevated vice-captaincy role.

"And that's what I really want. That's what I've asked and I'm really glad Steve is happy with that as well.

"We'll nut out exactly how that works, but it's going to be a real collaborative approach.

"It might look a bit different from the outside to other captains in the past, and that's great."

What if he needed to rest himself from the bowling load?

"I very much doubt if I will rest from Test cricket. I've never rested from Test cricket before and I doubt I will start now," Cummins said.

"(But) if I am injured or to miss a game, Steve would take over and it would be seamless."

That statement would be prophetic.

England's tour of Australia, led by Joe Root, was never going to be easy for the visitors and home side alike.

The world was still in the grip of the Covid-19 epidemic through 2021. Strict protocols were necessary for the tour to proceed.

For a time, the tour was in doubt as England did not want to be forced into sending a decimated team if Covid hit the squad before it left.

The tour only went ahead when England's demands for safeguards in Australia were met.

Australia's borders were closed at the time (October 2021) and special visas would be necessary. Biosecurity protocols had to be put in place. None of that was good news for the estimated 40,000 Australian citizens overseas who wanted to go home and had to wait.

Issues sorted as far as cricket was concerned at least, the England players and families arrived in November having been offered resort-

A COURAGEOUS DECISION

style accommodation on the Gold Coast as an initial hub. Families arriving for Christmas and the New Year served their quarantine at a Yarra Valley wine resort north-east of Melbourne.

As it turned out, the Australian team was first to run afoul of Covid, the victim being Pat Cummins due to close-contact protocols.

But his first match at the helm was a nine-wicket triumph for Australia at Brisbane's Gabba ground over December 8-12.

The Cummins record for the match: 7-89 (33.1 overs – 9 maidens, 155 dot balls); 12 runs in the first innings; did not bat in the second innings.

He was the first Australian to take a five-wicket haul in their first Test as captain since George Giffen in 1895. Other records: First captain since England's Bob Willis (1982) to get a five-wicket haul (5-38 off 13 overs) in an Ashes Test; first Australian captain to take a five-wicket haul since Michael Clarke in 2012; only the 11th bowler to take five wickets in a first innings as captain, and the only Australian to achieve that.

It was a glorious start for the rookie Test captain.

His spirits would have been high as the Australians headed to Adelaide for the second Test.

But the gods of misfortune had a hand to play. Cummins was at an Adelaide restaurant before the Test when another patron was identified as a positive Covid-19 case.

Protocols meant Cummins had to go into isolation. He took a PCR test that produced a negative result. But South Australia Health said because he was a close contact, he had to isolate for seven days, ruling him out of the pink-ball day-night Test at the Adelaide Oval.

Smith was elevated to the captaincy, a lot sooner than he would have thought likely, albeit for one match only. Australia won that Test and with Cummins back in charge went on to claim the series 4-0, one Test drawn.

How did the new skipper feel about such an impressive start? "It's madness. No way near what I could imagine my life would become as a young kid," he said.

He had enjoyed the captaincy, but what of his bowling?

One Australian who had a good idea about the captain's bowling performance was keeper Alex Carey.

"I just think his length is so good. He's challenging the batters' outside edge, he's challenging their inside edge," Carey said.

"He uses his bouncer really well. He charges in, he's hitting 140 (km/h) most deliveries and he digs in for big spells. It's pretty good leadership from our captain."

Of the 19 Australians to have taken 200 Test wickets, only Glenn McGrath (21.64) had a better bowling average than Cummins (22.53). None had a better strike-rate (46.89).

It is likely that many more people in England, India, Pakistan, South Africa, Sri Lanka, the West Indies and Bangladesh knew who was the Australian cricket team's captain than who led its Government.

Asked by Ron Reed to describe himself, not as a cricketer but pertaining to life in general, he said: "Pretty relaxed, pretty curious about different things. I try to have a lot of different things going on, whether it is in the business world, or meeting new people, interesting people. I find that really engaging and love it.

"I like to spend a lot of time with my family, try to have fun and not take anything too seriously."

It took some time for his appointment as captain to sink in. In a podcast he was asked, "When you're walking or at a cafe or just hanging out by yourself, do you ever just stop and go, 'Oh God, I'm the Australian cricket captain.' Does that happen to you?"

Cummins: "Yeah it does, does a little bit. It certainly did for the first few months when I became captain. I'd wake up in the morning going, 'Oh shit. What should an Australian captain do today? How should an Australian captain act?' Then I would kind of come back to going, 'I don't know. I have known a few captains. What did they do? I don't know them, I only know me,' And then I would kind of be like, 'Well, other people picked you.' So, I'm just going to do me until anyone tells me not to."

A COURAGEOUS DECISION

The first three years of his captaincy indicated that no one was going to be having such a conversation with him any time soon.

10

THE LONG RUN

Batting may be cricket's heartbeat, but fast bowling is it's pulse.
RODNEY HOGG, FORMER AUSTRALIAN FAST BOWLER, *SPEED THRILLS* (2015)

*If you haven't been a fast bowler you
haven't known the thrill of bowling bloody quick.*
AUSTRALIAN TEST LEGEND DENNIS LILLEE

Nobody would expect a fast bowler to have a long Test career, but one name stands out in fast bowling ranks for longevity.

England paceman James Anderson was still active off the long run-up at 41 years old. He played his last Test in 2024 after 20 years of Test cricket as England coach Brendon McCullum sought to get started on a new generation of fast bowlers.

Anderson's retirement came almost a year to the day after his long-time fast-bowling partner Stuart Broad packed up his cricket gear. Broad played 16 years of Test cricket and took 20 wickets in his last Ashes series, for the fifth time and two more than any other England bowler.

During the fifth Test (his 187th) away against India in March 2024, Anderson became the first fast bowler to take 700 Test wickets. Only two other bowlers had taken 700 Test wickets – spinners Muttiah Muralitharan (Sri Lanka) and Shane Warne (Australia).

Anderson was a rarity among fast bowlers, most of whom retreated to spectators' seating well before they got to 40.

To put that into some sort of context, Australia's most successful fast bowler has been Glenn McGrath, with 563 wickets in 124 matches. McGrath retired from Test cricket in January 2007 in the fifth Ashes Test against England in Sydney. He took a wicket with his last ball.

McGrath was 23 when he began his Test career and was 35 when he bowled that last ball in a Test, a month short of his 36th birthday.

A horror run with injury put Cummins out of the game for several years after he played his first Test in 2011 aged 18. He didn't play Test cricket again until around six years later.

Cummins said he needed to adjust mentally after forcing his way back into the Australian Test team in 2017 after almost six years on the outer.

"Cricket's basically 12 months of the year," he said in an interview in England.

"There's always a cricket game going on somewhere, and I played non-stop for a year or two.

"This is about four or five years ago, I kind of just came back from injuries.

"And I was just spent, like burnt out, and I just remember thinking, Jeez, I'm 25 here but I want to do this until I'm 35. I've got to find a way to balance all these different things."

He added to his workload by taking on extra T20 competition, including a return to the IPL in 2024 and signing up for Major League Cricket in the US.

An upside was that Australia didn't have any international cricket scheduled until the T20s and ODIs in England in September.

Did signing up in June 2024 to the MLC franchise San Francisco Unicorns give a hint to his plans?

His four-year deal would take him to 2027, possibly clashing with an Ashes tour in England. He would by then be 35, the age when fast bowlers seem to think about life after cricket.

Cummins had reckoned he could keep going until he was 35.

Cricket Australia requires its contracted players to give first priority to the national team.

The record of Cummins from the Tests he has played is impressive.

By March 2024 when he had turned 31, he had played 62 Tests, taking 269 wickets. That's averaging about 4.3 wickets per Test. McGrath's average over twice the number of Tests was around 4.5 wickets per Test.

A retirement age of 35 for fast bowlers seemed about right, Jimmy Anderson being an exception. Dennis Lillee was 35 when he retired from Test Cricket, as was his fast-bowling partner Jeff Thomson. So were English pacemen Bob Willis and John Snow. Stuart Broad was 37 when he called it a day in 2023.

Cummins did say, perhaps tongue in cheek, he'd retire when Nathan Lyon retired. Lyon was 37 at the time and had said he'd like to keep going until the 2027 Ashes.

Comparisons become tricky, however, as Test cricket was impacted by the advent of World Series back in the late 1970s and Covid in the 2020s. In 2003, T20 cricket started, adding yet another layer to the workload of cricketers.

Injuries would still be on Pat Cummins' mind as he plotted his future in the game.

He was well aware of what the cost of injuries could be. By the age of 23, he had suffered three stress fractures in his back and after his debut in 2011 it is calculated he missed around 60 Tests and something like 95 ODIs, before returning to the Test team in 2017.

According to Health and High Performance, a Melbourne based sports health specialist practice, lower back injuries represent around 20% of all cricket injuries.

In order, other injuries affected feet and ankles, wrist and fingers, knees, calf muscles, hamstrings, side and abdominal muscles.

Lower back injuries are attributed to bowling biomechanics, inadequate fitness, and high or sudden spikes in bowling workloads.

Cummins suffered mild right-side quadriceps soreness during a Test against the West Indies in 2022 and missed several sessions of play. He had just claimed his 200th Test wicket when he bowled rival skipper Kraigg Brathwaite, becoming the 19th Australian men's player to reach that mark and the first to do so with an average under 22 runs per wicket.

In July 2023 he injured a wrist in the fifth Ashes Test at The Oval in England and had to rest for six weeks. That meant he missed the tour to South Africa for short-form matches.

Having confessed to feeling "burnt out" not long after he returned from the run of injuries he suffered early in his career, just how long could he keep going in the demanding trade of fast bowling?

The Ashes series against England, either at home or away, would always be a priority.

He once wrote in an article for a cricket publication: "You know as a kid that the Ashes is extra special. It's not like other series. It's like a World Cup final every time it's played. The rich history, the story of the urn, the heroes and villains. It's one of those things that links cricket today back to a century ago."

Playing cricket in the 21st Century was practically a year-round occupation, internationally and domestically.

Not everyone played every game of course, but Australia's cricket schedule for 2024-25 looked like hard work for skipper Cummins, in Tests, ODI internationals and T20s.

In November 2024 Australia was to play Pakistan in three ODI matches. A five-Test series at home against India was to start in November and continue into 2025.

That meant Cummins most likely would be required for eight matches over two months. At least they would be at "home".

Australia completed a three-match Test series against Pakistan in January 2024, then hosted the West Indies for two Test matches and three ODIs. Then it was off to New Zealand for two Test matches. ODIs were to follow in Ireland and England from September.

Recent studies show that injury rates in cricket have increased with the advent of T20 cricket.

Research by Dr John Orchard, Chief Medical Officer for Cricket Australia and Cricket NSW, found that cricket injuries at elite level in Australia were occurring at a rate of around 18 injuries for a squad of 25 players who played 20 matches in a season. On average, around 9% of cricketers had an injury at any given time, although among fast bowlers that rate was significantly higher.

Dr Orchard noted the different physical demands involved in different types of cricket; the injury profile was slightly different between five-day Test matches and one-day matches. The launch of T20 cricket brought a new physical requirement.

Low back pain was particularly prevalent among younger fast bowlers, the research found. The repetitive action of bowling for long spells placed excessive stress on the tissues of the lower back, where stress fractures of the vertebra (spondylolysis) could develop.

Pat Cummins, and Cricket Australia, would be well aware of that.

Tours to the sub-continent would cause selection headaches as events in a series in Bangladesh in 2017 showed.

Cummins was the only fast bowler on that tour, coming just after his return to Test cricket and in weather with which players from Down Under would not be familiar.

In an article he wrote for *The Athlete's Voice* he described what he went through: "I was the only fast bowler in the Aussie XI. After the first over, it felt like I'd just completed a really, really hard fitness session. After the second over, it felt like I had done the hardest gym session of my life. After the third over, I just wanted to vomit.

"My mind was delirious. You're trying to force yourself to think, 'I've got to figure out a way to get the batsman out,' but, really, you're just wondering how you're going to get through the next over without falling in a heap.

"Every night I would go back to the hotel, crash and sleep for 12 hours straight.

"There was one day when we spent all three sessions in the field. Drinking fluids made me feel sick. I was taking anti-nausea tablets to try and keep the water down. It didn't work. I lost six-and-a-half kilos in a day.

"Sometimes, in between overs, I'd be at fine leg on all-fours vomiting. I didn't have a stomach bug. The conditions were just that harsh. There's no way to acclimatise to heat like that. You can't cool down. There's no breeze. Once you're hot, it's impossible to get your body temperature down.

"There were a few spells where the umpire, Ian Gould, was pretty much sending me off. He had suffered heat stroke before in India and was in hospital for a few days. Gunner would stop me after an over and say, 'You're not bowling any more. You're having an ice bath!'

"When I look back on it all, it makes me happy. That might sound like a strange thing to say – it certainly wasn't much fun at the time! – but I'm really satisfied that I got through it all."

Cummins was only 24 at that time.

Now in his 30s, his workload would have to be carefully monitored if he was to stay on the pitch as a lethal fast bowler until he was 35. Cricket, after all, is a summer game.

Fear of burnout was the reason Cricket Australia gave for omitting Cummins from the white-ball squad to tour England and Scotland in 2024.

PAT CUMMINS

OLDEST TEST CRICKETERS ON FINAL APPEARANCE

NAME	COUNTRY	DOB	TEST DEBUT	LAST MATCH	AGE AT LAST TEST
Wilfred Rhodes	England	29 October 1877	1 June 1899	12 April 1930	52 years, 165 days
Bert Ironmonger	Australia	7 April 1882	30 November 1928	28 February 1933	50 years, 327 days
WG Grace	England	18 July 1848	6 September 1880	3 June 1899	50 years, 320 days
George Gunn	England	13 June 1879	13 December 1907	12 April 1930	50 years, 303 days
James Southerton	England	16 November 1827	15 March 1877	4 April 1877	49 years, 139 days
Miran Bakhsh	Pakistan	20 April 1907	29 January 1955	16 February 1955	47 years, 302 days
Sir Jack Hobbs	England	16 December 1882	1 January 1908	22 August 1930	47 years, 249 days
Frank Woolley	England	27 May 1887	9 August 1909	22 August 1934	47 years, 87 days
Don Blackie	Australia	5 April 1882	14 December 1928	8 February 1929	46 years, 309 days
Bert Strudwick	England	28 January 1880	1 January 1910	18 August 1926	46 years, 202 days

None of those played beyond 1955. None were express bowlers (Jack Hobbs) was a medium-pacer. Source: *Cricinfo*.

11

CAN BOWL, CAN BAT, CAN FIELD

Some more conventional wisdom: to be considered an all-rounder in cricket your batting average must be higher than your bowling average.

In his first year back in Test Cricket, 2017, both averages for Pat Cummins were so close he could almost lay claim to being a genuine all-rounder – 237 runs at 26.33 and 29 wickets at 29.79.

Bowling is his forte. One coach noted: "His ability to consistently bowl at high speeds with accuracy and control is a key factor in his success. He has a smooth run-up, a clean action, and a strong wrist position that allows him to generate pace and movement off the pitch."

Clearly, he was first selected in the Test team as a bowler, but he could wield a bat when the chips were down.

Those wishing to classify him as an all-rounder point to his numbers but his role as captain is a factor that cannot be overlooked in all-round attributes.

He has played a few "captain's knocks" as the saying goes, that have helped Australia out of strife.

In an Ashes Test match in 2023 as Australia chased down a target of 282 runs, Cummins scored 44 not out from 73 balls.

His stoic resistance saw Australia emerge from looming defeat in a 2013 World Cup ODI final to reach the final against India in India…and win it.

Maybe an all-purpose combination is preferable to a single all-rounder in modern Test cricket. As one scribe wrote mid-way through Cummins' first Ashes series as captain in 2021: "He certainly is no one-trick pony. In the first two Tests he has bowled superbly, batted impressively and fielded as well as anyone."

That held true through that series and into those that followed, home and away.

In the April 2024 ICC rankings (based on a pointscore system), Cummins appeared on the all-rounder list at No. 8. At the top was Ravindra Jadeja, of India. Cummins' teammates Mitchell Starc, Cameron Green and Nathan Lyon made it, at Nos 14, 15 and 17 respectively.

Cummins' averages in 2011, then from 2017 to 2024, might show that his batting has declined (over many more innings of course) but his bowling has improved greatly. It must be remembered that in 2017 he was returning to Test cricket after an absence of six years.

Up to June 2024, he had played 62 Tests: 269 wickets at an average of 22.53 (best 10-69); 1,295 runs at an average of 17.03 (highest score 64 not out).

His highest score was a rearguard action against the West Indies in Brisbane in 2024. Cummins went to the wicket with Australia at 7-161, 150 runs behind the West Indies' first innings total. He faced a barrage of short-pitched bowling early and had to wear a few hits. But he held on to remain not out.

Wicketkeeper Alex Carey was full of praise for his skipper. "Amazing cricketer, isn't he?" he said after the day's play.

"I think that's probably the best I've seen him bat.

"(It was) a bit of a counterpunch as well, he got bombarded early with some short stuff and then found a way through and was able to play some really good shots."

A bold declaration while still behind eventually saw Australia lose the match by just eight runs.

On the basis of "conventional wisdom" Cummins is not a genuine all-rounder, but would certainly qualify as a bowling all-rounder, usually batting at No. 8 or 9.

CAN BOWL, CAN BAT, CAN FIELD

There's one unusual stat that is worth noting.

Cummins' average of 33.6 in the usually-decisive fourth innings of Test matches is better than nearly all of Australia's top-order batters.

Obviously, he has a few more "not outs" to his name than the top order but in runs per innings he compares favourably.

AUSTRALIA: BATTING IN THE 4TH INNINGS (TO JUNE 2024)

	Innings	Average	Runs/Inns
Pat Cummins	12	33.6	19.6
Steve Smith	29	33.3	26.4
Usman Khawaja	26	29.8	26.3
Marnus Labuschagne	14	29.8	19.1
Cameron Green	4	25.0	18.8
Mitchell Marsh	18	19.2	18.1

That doesn't make him an all-rounder but does make him an all-purpose player. He doesn't usually field in the catching positions behind the wicket, but he has 32 Test catches to his name.

One of his best innings came in the 2023 Ashes Test in Birmingham when his 44 not out helped Australia chase down 281.

And another point: Cummins had hit the winning run in three Australian successful chases of 250 or more.

That record began in South Africa in 2011 when Cummins capped off an amazing Test debut, hitting the winning runs with a four over mid-wicket and taking seven wickets for the match with his electrifying pace. He was a deserved man-of-the match. A decade later he did it again, scoring the winning runs in Tests against New Zealand and England.

The latter two efforts were those of a batsman determined to be there for victory. It was a little different in South Africa when he joined Mitchell Johnson at the crease.

Cummins explained, with a grin: "Mitch asked me to keep a cool head and I took that for swinging."

The first session had been lost to rain and after five days Cummins was at the crease; Australia's chances had come down to him with only two wickets in hand.

When Greg Chappell had first seen Cummins play, he thought he could develop into a genuine all-rounder. Perhaps in South Africa his batting could save the day for Australia after his stellar bowling effort.

Cummins took strike and waited for a ball that he could hit. He got it and smashed it to the boundary.

He was an instant hero, but that shot probably was not in the armoury of a genuine allrounder. Nobody cared much, he was being celebrated as a future star of the game. Maybe even an all-rounder.

Australia has spent many seasons trying to find a genuine all-rounder to fit into the Test team; someone akin to Sir Ian Botham in his heyday who could take wickets and amass runs.

Botham averaged 33.55 for his 5,200 runs and 28.40 for his 383 wickets; he sits third on England's all-time wickets list behind Anderson and Broad.

According to ratings by *crictracker.com* these have been the Top 10 all-rounders in Test cricket:

1. Sir Gary Sobers (West Indies)
2. Jacques Kallis (South Africa)
3. Kapil Dev (India)
4. Imran Khan (Pakistan)
5. Sir Richard Hadlee (New Zealand)
6. Sir Ian Botham (England)
7. Wally Hammond (England)
8. Andrew Flintoff (England)
9. Shaun Pollock (South Africa)
10. Richie Benaud (Australia)

CAN BOWL, CAN BAT, CAN FIELD

None are still active. Only two, (Sir) Garfield Sobers and Jacques Kallis, have batting averages that are 20 greater than their bowling averages over their entire careers. They were genuine all-rounders.

Says crictracker.com: "A good all-rounder is a must in making a champion team and most of these all-rounders played a crucial role in their country's domination in the format...They bring about a balance in the side which allows the captain to play an extra seamer or batsman and no great side in cricket has worked its way up without a top-class all-rounder."

At the top of the list (Sir) Garfield Sobers played in 93 Tests, 1954-74. He scored 8,032 runs at an average of 57.78; he took 235 wickets at an average of 34.03.

Richie Benaud at No. 10 on the list played 63 Tests (1952-64). He scored 2,201 runs at an average of 24.45; he took 248 wickets at an average of 27.03. Close to genuine but looking like a bowling all-rounder.

Left-arm paceman Alan Davidson, played 44 Tests for Australia from 1953-63. He took 186 Test wickets at an average of 20.53 and scored 1,328 Test runs at an average 24.59. A genuine all-rounder, you might say. A side note: Davidson's bowling record in the sub-continent was unsurpassed by any visiting paceman, 44 wickets at 17.86 from 10 tests on spinning wickets.

That was then. How about now?

All-rounders have a place in Test cricket but are particularly valuable in the short forms, in ODIs particularly.

All-rounders in T20 have different DNA. The problem for all-rounders in T20 is that they are likely to see a lot of their bowling disappear over the fence or at least to the boundary ropes that are much in use these days. And they are expected to return the favour if they get a turn to bat. Bowlers are not, after all, expected to bat for the full 20 overs – they need to get runs, quickly, from what might only be a couple of overs at most, even the last ball or two.

Test cricket almost always requires a different approach from all-rounders – someone who can take wickets and restrict scoring, then score runs usually in conjunction with a recognised batter or hold up an end with a bowler at the tail of the field.

Mitchell Marsh seemed the most likely candidate for all-rounder but he was in and out of the Test squad, due mostly to injuries.

The arrival on the scene of another West Australian, Cameron Green, in 2023, put a new name on the list of "possibles."

Marsh's Test record: 42 matches, 2,010 runs at an average of 30.45 (highest score 181); 48 wickets at an average 40.04. Again, according to conventional wisdom, he'd be a bowling all-rounder.

Cameron Greens statistics (Test debut in 2020) are worth noting: 28 Tests, 1,377 runs at an average of 36.23 (highest score 174 not out); 35 wickets at an average of 35.31.

On those numbers, the emergence of Green could be the answer to the search for a genuine all-rounder when Marsh is done. Like Cummins, however, he had early problems with stress fractures in his back.

Since recovering, Green has been a force in all three forms of international cricket.

Interestingly, Cummins has spoken of Mitchell Starc as an all-rounder.

Starc's statistics: 89 Tests, 2,093 runs at an average of 20.5; 368 wickets at an average of 27.7. A bowling all-rounder.

But as noted, statistics don't always tell the true story. At what stage of an innings runs are scored and wickets taken is more meaningful in Test cricket than averages might indicate.

An Australian captain (former) who himself would not claim to be a genuine all-rounder but whose efforts with the ball yielded results at crucial times in Tests is Allan Border.

Twice, he took five wickets in an innings, and once 10 wickets in a match.

He scored 11,174 runs at an average of 50.65 before he retired in 1994. He took 39 wickets at an average of 39.10 (best 7-46).

CAN BOWL, CAN BAT, CAN FIELD

Border's bowling career is worth mentioning in the context of performance at critical times.

His seven-wicket return had the mighty West Indies reeling during the Sydney Test in 1989.

The West Indies crushed Australia in Brisbane, Perth and Melbourne before the SCG match.

Viv Richards won the toss and decided to bat. Gordon Greenidge and Desmond Haynes handled the bowling attack of Terry Alderman, Merv Hughes, and spinners Peter Taylor and Trevor Hohns with apparent ease.

Border recalled: "I looked at the scoreboard, and things weren't going that well and I think I might have looked at Steve Waugh who said 'why don't you have a bowl'.

"I was looking around for answers and I thought, surely not me, surely I don't have to come on.

"We were struggling, I made the decision to come on and bowl…I am just letting them go, I'm not sure what's going to happen."

Border dismissed Richie Richardson (28) early in his spell with the West Indies at 2-144. Another massive total still looked likely.

But the wicket of Richardson sparked a collapse, as Border took seven wickets as eight West Indies batsmen were out for only 80 runs, all out for 224. Australia went on to win by seven wickets.

Teammates said some of the balls that got wickets were not all that great.

Border conceded: "I was getting a fair bit of bagging I have got to say, you know things like 'shit does get wickets occasionally'."

One of his players, Steve Waugh, later to be a captain himself who bowled a bit, said of Border: "Allan was a reluctant bowler, which was a shame because he was a much better spin bowler than he gave himself credit for."

Border was "as good as anyone" at exploiting a spin-friendly wicket, Waugh said.

Pat Cummins of course does not have to wonder if he should bowl

PAT CUMMINS

at all, or not. He just has to decide when he will bowl.

As captain of Australia's ODI team, Cummins needs to be astute. Results suggest he is.

He had played 88 ODIs to June 2024, having batted in only 57. Australia had won 80% of the matches in which he was captain.

Cummins' 141 ODI wickets came at an average of 28.66 (best 5-71). He scored 497 runs (highest 37) at an average of 13.66, coming in late in an innings usually with little time to make an impression.

As noted, T20 cricket is a different beast.

In the international game where a "par" score is at least 170 on most wickets, bowlers usually come off worst.

In the 2021 T20 World Cup, teams batting second won almost twice as many matches as teams batting first in the 45 matches.

Leaving aside the Indian Premier League for this exercise, Cummins until the 2024 T20I World Cup had taken 55 wickets at an average of 24.54 and with an economy rate (average number of runs per over bowled) of 7.37 in his 50-game career in T20I matches.

Each bowler only gets four overs in T20 which means they can cop a lot of stick. Only one fast bowler figured in the top 10 economy rates in T20I into 2024, India's Jasprit Bumrah (6.63). Indian spinner Ravindra Jadeja had the best economy rate, 6.35 runs conceded per over.

New Zealander Daniel Vettori retired in 2014 but his record in T20 internationals became the benchmark for bowlers. He played 34 matches, bowling 131.1 overs at an economy rate of 5.70, the only bowler then to have an economy rate less than 6.0.

By trade, Pat Cummins is a fast bowler, and even after that stunning debut in 2011 he still ranks among the world's best whether it be Tests or ODIs.

• • •

What is it like to face a rampant Pat Cummins, a projectile coming your way at 145-150 km/h, even wearing all the protective gear that's available from helmets to all-over padding?

You wouldn't leave home without it.

CAN BOWL, CAN BAT, CAN FIELD

One batsman who well-knows is Pakistan's Babar Azam. In 2024, he was ranked the No. 1 ODI batsmen in world cricket, No.3 in Test cricket and No. 4 in T20Is.

He had faced Cummins many times (for 208 balls according to statisticians) and he was on the end of one of Cummins' unplayable thunderbolts in the Boxing Day Test in Melbourne in 2023. He'd earlier copped another "peach" in the Perth Test.

In Melbourne, Pakistan won the toss and sent Australia in. The home side made 318 runs, certainly "gettable". Pakistan in reply was 2-124 when Babar Azam arrived at the wicket. He scored one run before Cummins nailed him.

Just as Pakistan's batters looked as if they might get on top for the first time in the series, Cummins grabbed two wickets in four balls to steal the momentum back for Australia.

The ball that got Babar Azam was a highlight of the series.

Just weeks earlier in Perth, Babar also fell victim to Cummins, having been set up brilliantly.

Five months later back in Pakistan in an interview on a local news channel Babar was asked about the best bowlers he'd faced.

Cummins was the toughest he said, followed by Jasprit Bumrah (India), Mark Wood (England), and Mitchell Starc (Australia).

He said Cummins' attribute was "skilfulness" – he was consistently improving and never offered loose deliveries. Cummins, he said, had the ability to strategically trap batsmen, making every delivery a challenge.

"The way he has, over the years, improved, he will not give you a loose ball," Babar said. "He knows how he can take the wicket of a certain batter by bowling at a certain position. He traps you. He gives you a tough time. He challenges your tempering and technique to the fullest."

Babar mentioned Cummins' ability to vary pace. He also suggested that Cummins was precise in his length; any variation was deliberate, aimed at unsettling a batsman.

"If he does a loose bowl, then I think that he does that intentionally,"

Babar said. "That is why I rate him highly because he has the ability to take a wicket. He never bowls with a consistent pace; he would normally bowl at 130-135 and then suddenly bowl you out at 145. So he has that ability to vary his pace. One thing about him is that he will always bowl at hard length; if he is bowling at full length, then it is intentional."

• • •

He doesn't field in the slips but that doesn't mean Pat Cummins isn't a chance to take a wicket when he's in the outfield.

He's had his share of drops, just has almost every cricketer at elite level under the pressure that goes with the game.

But when it comes to throwing down the wickets he can be as good as the best from a distance.

An effort in 2018 at Adelaide Oval in a Test match against India would take beating, maybe even the "best run-out ever" as commentator Adam Gilchrist exclaimed on *Fox Sports*.

It was Day 1 of the first Test against India, close to 6pm Adelaide time and around two minutes from the end of the day's play.

Cummins had bowled 19 overs from his 20 metres run-up. It was about 39 degrees. Drinks, anyone?

Indian No. 3 Cheteshwar Pujara had reached 123 runs and obviously was hoping to see out the day undefeated.

Josh Hazelwood bowled to him. Pujara drove the ball towards mid-wicket and set off for a somewhat cheeky single, possibly thinking that Pat Cummins wasn't the most dangerous fielder.

He was wrong. Cummins swooped on the ball like an MCG seagull on a hot chip, scooped it up one-handed and in mid-air pinged at the stumps (he probably would have only been able to see one stump from side-on) while he was twisting and diving.

The ball clattered into the stumps. Pujara was about a metre short of his ground. That was the end of him, and the day's play.

Sadly for Australia, India won the Test by 31 runs.

But the replays of the run-out is still a *YouTube* hit.

CAN BOWL, CAN BAT, CAN FIELD

Cummins is no slouch in the field. He has 32 Test, 15 ODI and 4 T20I catches to his name.

TRIVIA: Two Australians have been knighted for services to cricket. One was Sir Donald Bradman. Who was the other? Answer at the back of the book.

12

CLOSING THE 'GATE

Internet 101: Comments on social media platforms should not be taken as representative of public opinion.

Social media can sometimes be more of a platform for rants by people who otherwise would not enjoy even one moment of fame rather than contribute a reasoned discussion of issues.

This is particularly so when it comes to such divisive topics that occupy the minds of some fans of cricket, football, basketball and other sports.

Social media is a strange place when it comes to football, in England for example. There is a proliferation of so-called fan sites, many of which probably are fake. The giveaways as to voracity include the strange names used by those who post comments and the criticism levelled at players, managers and owners. Sack the manager, sack the player, sack the owner are common threats by so-called fans.

What seem to be facts are often fake news.

Cricket fans by and large are a more conservative lot, but social media has given voice to armchair critics who might otherwise have expressed their views in the local pub.

There aren't many controversial incidents in world cricket. That's not saying there are none.

Of course, Australian cricket was in the firing line in 2018 with the "sandpaper-gate" affair that came to light in South Africa. And social media as well as the mainstream press and media (at home and abroad) lit up.

CLOSING THE 'GATE

Former Australia captain Michael Clarke, was one of many who could not believe what had happened. He tweeted: "WHAT THE........ HAVE I JUST WOKEN UP TO. Please tell me this is a bad dream."

Retired Test bowling great Shane Warned joined in on Twitter: "Very disappointed with the pictures I saw on our coverage here in Cape Town. If proven the alleged ball tampering is what we all think it is, then I hope Steve Smith (Captain) & Darren Lehmann (Coach) do the press conference to clean this mess up!"

There was little to no social media support for the Australians involved, at least initially. The mood changed later amid a smattering of calls for bans and suspensions to be eased or even lifted.

The scandal that engulfed the Australian cricket team left the public deeply hurt. Even a group of boys at a Melbourne primary school vowed they wouldn't play cricket because Australia "cheated." Hopefully, they've put that in the past and now enjoy the cricket played by Australia since then.

Three players were singled out by Cricket Australia for the South African incident – captain Steve Smith, his deputy David Warner and batter Cameron Bancroft – and were dealt severe penalties.

This wasn't a case of picking at a seam or using a sticky lolly to affect the movement of the ball. And it wasn't as first claimed – the use of grit and sticky tape. It was sandpaper, taken on to the field for a particular purpose.

The fallout went far beyond ball-tampering, given the seniority of the players involved, granted that Bancroft was found to be the junior partner in the plot.

The reaction in Australia went all the way top the top – then-Prime Minister Malcolm Turnbull called the episode a "shocking disappointment" and urged Cricket Australia to take "decisive action."

"The whole nation is shocked," he said, " because they hold those who wear the baggy green to be on a pedestal; as high as you can get in Australia, certainly higher than any politician."

Smith and Warner were stood down from their roles for the

remainder of the Newlands Test. They and Bancroft were then suspended and sent home.

Cricket Australia then banned Smith and Warner for 12 months. The BCCI (India's cricket authority) also banned them from the IPL. Bancroft was given a nine-month penalty.

Cricket Australia found Warner initiated the plan and was told he would never again be considered for a leadership position within the Australian team.

CA found Smith had known about the plot but failed to prevent it. He would not be eligible for a leadership role until a year after his ban expired on March 29, 2019. He was therefore able to be appointed deputy to Pat Cummins in 2021.

Bancroft's ban cost him a contract with Somerset in the UK County championship.

Coach Darren Lehmann was found to be clear of any wrongdoing but revealed his intention to stand down after the South Africa series: "It is the right time to step away," Lehmann said. "I hope the team rebuilds and the Australian public can forgive the young men and get behind the XI."

Later, a review into the culture of Cricket Australia found that the organisation was "arrogant".

Australian fans didn't seem too concerned about Cricket Australia, but many had opinions on the three who were banned, particularly the two from the leadership group.

Social media was alight with calls, on the one-hand for lifetime bans from representing Australia, to those who thought the one-year bans were way too harsh in view of other ball-tampering penalties in world cricket.

Bowlers Cummins, Hazlewood, Lyon and Starc were unscathed by CA's inquiry, but that didn't stop idle speculation they might have known what was going on. Past players were among those asking questions. "They must have known" was a theme among some critics.

The four bowlers saw fit to issue a public statement criticising the

CLOSING THE 'GATE

questioning of their integrity and requesting "an end to the rumour-mongering and innuendo".

Cricket Australia backed the bowlers.

David Warner kept the episode in the limelight through 2022 when he sought to have his leadership ban revoked.

CA set up an independent process for players and staff seeking to review long-term bans, Warner asking for his "life" sanction be overturned.

An independent three-person panel was to consider his case, but on the eve of Australia's second Test against the West Indies, Warner said he had withdrawn his application to the review panel because he was not prepared to subject his family or team-mates to "further trauma and disruption."

There was something of turnover of personnel at Cricket Australia, though not all related to "sandpaper-gate". High-performance manager Pat Howard and senior executive Ben Amarfio were pushed out of their roles. CEO James Sutherland, CA chairman David Peever and long-time board member Mark Taylor resigned to create a "fresh start" for cricket administration.

Was that the end of it? All three banned players returned to cricket, Warner's restriction still in force, and the world seemed to move on.

But English fans weren't about to let things fade away. The Bairstow run-out in the Ashes series in 2023 rekindled the rage of fans, and the media.

Outlets such as Twitter (now X) were besieged by protests, a vast majority from English fans and non-fans. It is fair to say that in this case there was solid support by most Australians for their players; maybe it was it just an anti-Pom thing?

The Australian players in the Lord's Ashes Test were greeted with boos and cries of "Aussie! Aussie! Aussie! Cheat! Cheat! Cheat!" and "Same old Aussies, always cheating!"

The wounds were still there, although for the Australians it seemed to be water off the duck's back as far as one could tell from their demeanour, at least initially. The Bairstow run-out got them fired up when players were abused by a few members in the Long Room at Lord's.

The incident resulted in one Marylebone Cricket Club (MCC) member banned for life and another two suspended for "abusive, offensive or inappropriate behaviour or language."

Warner seemed to put it all behind him but in 2023 announced he'd be retiring; he'd bow out of Test cricket in 2023 and out of the short-form games after the 2024 T20 World Cup.

Smith continued in the role of deputy to Pat Cummins, filling in as captain when Covid sidelined the skipper in the Adelaide Ashes Test and again when Cummins left the Indian tour early to be with his ailing mother.

Bancroft returned to cricket ahead of the other two and was building an impressive portfolio of scores in the Sheffield Shield for his West Australian team.

When Warner announced his retirement from Test cricket, Bancroft should have thought he was a good chance to return to the Test fold.

But a phone call from Cummins put an end to those dreams.

Cummins rang Bancroft to tell him he wasn't in the squad for the series against the West Indies in January 2024, despite being the dominant scorer in the past two seasons of the Sheffield Shield.

Cummins was said to have made it clear his non-selection in the Test squad had nothing to do with the sandpaper saga.

Bancroft had returned from his suspension to open the batting for Australia in the 2019 Ashes but was dropped after two Tests.

Former Test player and West Australian Tom Moody was one to question Bancroft's non-selection, asking whether there was an "agenda" in the call.

Moody on social media: "Selection is never an easy task but the oversight of Cameron Bancroft is shocking. His first-class numbers are so compelling against his peers it feels there is another agenda which I hope was communicated to him honestly!"

CLOSING THE 'GATE

Bancroft's Test record was 18 innings for 446 runs at an average of 26.3. Probably not enough to hold an opening role – he needed to continue get runs in the domestic Sheffield Shield competition and even in County cricket in England where he was playing for Gloucestershire where early in the season he was averaging 48.4.

For his part, Bancroft said in 2023 he had paid his dues over the sandpaper saga although some his remarks indicated he hadn't entirely "let it go."

Chairman of selectors George Bailey said the bowlers from Newlands had not had any say in Bancroft's non-selection.

"Categorically no. And I've shared this with Cameron on a number of occasions," he said.

"It has never at any stage been discussed from the panel's perspective. It's purely a cricketing decision.

"There's not a member of the team that would have an issue with Cam playing. We certainly don't have an issue with it.

"A lot of people tend to forget the fact that Cam has actually played Test cricket since returning from the ban. It was a long time ago.

"We've all moved well past that. I'd be disappointed if people were looking to that as a reason. That's not the case. Never has been and never will be."

It provoked a degree of uproar in WA when it was revealed Steve Smith would become Usman Khawaja's opening partner.

Former coach Justin Langer weighed in: "Others might point to his past, and a vast error of judgment in South Africa. He, like no other, knows the mistake he made. He has taken major steps forward, just as Steve Smith and David Warner did after their suspensions. Hopefully he has been forgiven for that."

• • •

Injury-hit India chased down 328 to inflict on Australia its first Test defeat in Brisbane since 1988 and win one of the all-time great series 2-1 back in 2021, an upset by most measures.

It was only India's second ever series win in Australia in more than a dozen visits since the first in 1947-48. Questions were asked about the side that was under the direction of Tim Paine.

There was a personal upside for Cummins in that series. He took the most wickets (21) and was named player of a remarkable 2021 series.

First, India was bowled out for just 36 runs in the first Test in Adelaide. Australia won that Test but lost two others at the MCG and the Gabba. The SCG Test was drawn.

The decider was at the Gabba in Brisbane. Australia had made the ground its own; it was even referred to as the "Gabbatoir". The ground's usually lively green-tops had been a graveyard for visiting teams, especially those from the sub-continent where such greenery was usually only seen in grazing lands.

India's series-clinching victory there was widely described as one of their greatest wins ever. (The West Indies added to Australia's Gabba agony in 2024, then on Pat Cummins' watch).

Trouble had been brewing in the Australian camp before the series loss to India. It isn't clear whether the behind-the-scenes goings-on affected the on-field performance of the Australians. Cricket fans would think Australia would be better than that.

The rumblings centred on coach Justin Langer, a former Test batsman, who took over the squad from Darren Lehman after "sandpaper-gate."

The rumblings were reaching a crescendo by August 2021 when the noise was loud enough to force Cricket Australia to step in, with then chairman Earl Eddings and CEO Nick Hockley meeting captains Paine and Aaron Finch (limited overs) and vice-captain Cummins.

Langer's contract was due to expire in 2022. Obviously some sort of review would occur before a new contract was put on the table.

But the rumblings, aired in the press that quoted unnamed sources, seemed to disturb the Cricket Australia hierarchy.

Ron Reed wrote in *Captain Pat*: "It was revealed that some senior players were unhappy with coach Justin Langer's management style.

CLOSING THE 'GATE

"Few, if any, names were mentioned, but journalists with their ear to the ground as it became a major talking point correctly arrived at the conclusion that Cummins was one of them, a weighty factor if true given that he was vice-captain of the Test and white-ball teams.

"It meant that he had to participate in an investigation in which the then chairman of the CA board, Earl Eddings, and the Chief Executive, Nick Hockley, quizzed him and white-ball captain Aaron Finch about the allegations of unrest. Langer was given the thumbs up to carry on, but the uneasiness lingered."

The cracks started to appear in early 2021 when the Channel Nine newspapers, the *Sydney Morning Herald* and *The Age*, leaked information that players weren't seeing eye to eye with the coach. They'd apparently found him and his methods to be overbearing and intense, something that seemed at odds with what Cummins was later to say in a long statement he penned.

Some of Australia's greatest Test players of the modern era, including Mark Waugh, Adam Gilchrist, Ricky Ponting, Steve Waugh, Matthew Hayden and Shane Warne criticised Cricket Australia for the way it treated Langer.

Hockley released a statement praising the job Langer had performed in "raising the culture, values and behaviours" of the team. It was just an uneasy truce.

Langer began to take a more background role, delegating more responsibility to assistant coaches during the T20 World Cup and the Ashes.

From then, the team lost only one match, early in the World Cup.

Despite celebrating win after win, the players – Cummins included most likely – were not convinced that Langer was capable of sustaining his new approach if things started to "go south."

The only conclusion was that players – at least some of them – wanted him out. Was that a unanimous view? Who knows?

As Cummins repeatedly said, it wasn't his or his team's call to make, and until it was made, until due process was carried out, anything they said – for or against – had the potential to inflame a delicate and uncertain situation.

Whatever process Cricket Australia went through, Langer was offered only a short-term extension of his contract, enough to get Australia through the T20 World Cup.

Despite winning the T20 World Cup and a 4-0 win over England to regain the Ashes, Langer was only offered a six-month extension. He decided he'd had enough and fell on his sword.

He left quietly at the time, with dignity, as many commentators observed. He bided his time before launching an attack on the handling of the situation, referring to "politics" within CA.

Similarly, Cummins waited a while before having his say.

He had acknowledged that Langer "tweaked his coaching style" after the crisis meeting with CA and "did a really, really good job". But, he said, said the playing group had questioned whether the changes were sustainable long term. Maybe it was the right time for a different direction.

Cummins said Cricket Australia had made a "brave call" in only offering Langer a short-term contract extension but said the playing group would have accepted whatever decision was made.

Speaking long after the dust settled, Langer said: "Ironically, the last six months of my coaching career were the most enjoyable period of 12 years. Not only did we win everything, but I had energy, and I had focus, and I was happy – besides the politics."

Former player Victorian Andrew McDonald took over from Langer whose coaching career moved on. Langer and former captain Ricky Ponting were sounded out in 2024 for the coaching job with the Indian team but declined. Both were coaching in the Indian Premier League at the time, Langer with Lucknow Super Giants and Ponting with Delhi Capitals. Both teams failed to make the 2024 IPL play-offs.

Ponting had said he might be interested in the Australian coaching job "someday".

Cricket Australia opted for one head coach for all formats. McDonald was pleased about that. One of his assistant coaches was former New Zealand Test spinner Daniel Vettori.

"The great challenge for coaches and players is to manage your workload," McDonald said.

"I'd like to think that I've got coaching staff around who can step up. We can elevate certain coaches at different times to take on different tours and different challenges.

"So some coaches will get exposed along the journey to help out the workload, which is quite significant for a head coach.

"Where it's landed, (I'm) very comfortable, where it's landed, and what it looks like."

• • •

Tim Paine was gone from the Test team in 2021 amid a texting scandal. He had taken over as captain in 2018 and retired from first class cricket in March 2023.

At a press conference to announce that he was stepping down as captain, Paine described it as "an incredibly difficult decision but the right one for me, my family and cricket."

He said: "Although exonerated, I deeply regretted this incident at the time and still do today.

"I spoke to my wife and family at the time and am enormously grateful for their forgiveness and support.

"On reflection, my actions in 2017 do not meet the standard of an Australian cricket captain, or the wider community."

Paine had been considering retirement at the start of the 2017-18 season but was talked out of it, progressing eventually to keeping wicket for the Test team.

He played 35 Tests for Australia after his debut against Pakistan at Lord's in 2010. After playing in four Tests that year, he did not return to Australia's Test squad until the 2017-18 Ashes.

Paine's place behind the stumps went to Alex Carey. Cummins and McDonald became the custodians of Australia's re-built cricket reputation.

PAT CUMMINS

Paine made a comeback to playing the game, albeit briefly, at club level amid rumours in 2022 that he'd also been training with the Tasmanian team with an eye to a place in the state's Sheffield Shield team. On 17 March 2023, Paine announced his retirement from cricket. He later took on a coaching role with the Adelaide Strikers in the Big Bash competition and a part-time coaching role with the Australian Under-19 and Australia A teams.

He also expressed an interest in a future head-coach role, something to which Cummins believed he would be well-suited.

"Painey would be a great coach I think," Cummins said. "One of his strengths that I loved when he was captain was he's a great people manager. He knows how to get the best out of every player. He brings the team close together.

"He's played a lot of cricket, he's seen a lot of cricket, he deals with people brilliantly."

The key figures in the "sandpaper-gate" controversy served their penalties and returned to active cricket. Warner and Smith were taken back into the Australian side, Warner still prohibited from a leadership role and closing the door on his Australian career in 2024.

Smith took on the role of opener in the Test team after Warner's retirement, not overwhelmingly successful, it must be said, for at least three of his four efforts (12, 11 not out, 6). His best was a 91 not out against the West Indies at the Gabba in January 2024 which came oh-so-close to helping Australia grab an unlikely win.

Smith received ringing endorsement from teammate Nathon Lyon: "We're talking about arguably the greatest player in the last decade. There's a lot of talk about his batting. I sit here and laugh because he's arguably the best problem-solver I've ever played with."

Smith's batting record from his Test debut in 2010 to 2024 spoke for itself: 108 Tests; 9,685 runs at an average of 56.97; top score 239; 32 centuries.

The 35-year-old would need some more good numbers to retain his role as opener, perhaps even his place in the team.

CLOSING THE 'GATE

Cameron Bancroft resumed his cricket career with the Perth Scorchers in the 2018 Big Bash competition and returned to the Test team for the Ashes tour in England in 2019. He was dropped after failing to produce big scores. He joined Durham in the English County Championship in 2019 and signed for Gloucestershire in 2024. He began amassing the big scores he was going to need to impress Australia's selectors for a possible return as opener. In one match he scored 53 and 130 not out.

The Australian team settled into the task of consigning "sandpaper-gate", sexting and apparent player discontent to the dust of the past.

Future controversies most likely would centre on what happened on the pitch, not behind the scenes.

13

IT'S JUST NOT CRICKET

In July 2023, Australia held on in day five of the Lord's Test to claim a 43-run victory and 2-0 lead in the Ashes series with the old foe, England.

The match produced one of the biggest controversies in modern Test cricket (according to the English press at least), leaving aside the sandpaper scandal in South Africa five years earlier and any number of other incidents.

In the Lord's match, England wicketkeeper/batter Johnny Bairstow walked out of his crease after ducking Cameron Green's last delivery of an over. The ball sailed through to Australian keeper Alex Carey who immediately underarmed the ball at the wicket to have a wandering Bairstow stumped.

The bemused Bairstow, last recognised batsman in the England line-up, was sent back to the pavilion. The Australians refused to call him back.

Several unsavoury incidents followed. Carey wore abuse for many months after the incident, even though it emerged that the stumping was the idea of skipper Cummins.

Television footage showed confrontation between spectators and players in the Long Room as Australians Usman Khawaja and David Warner passed through on their way to lunch.

The Marylebone Cricket Club dealt with three members over the Long Room incidents.

And there was a heated exchange when England paceman Stuart Broad confronted the Australian skipper on the field.

IT'S JUST NOT CRICKET

Broad said afterwards in his social media podcast: "As I'm walking out to bat at Lord's and there's boos going at the Aussies, the captain Pat Cummins is coming on to bowl, so he's walking towards me at the end of his mark.

"And I just looked at him and said, 'You're an absolute disgrace'.

"He said, 'Oh yeah, you're hardly an upkeep of the spirit of cricket'."

Cummins was referring to an incident in the 2013 Ashes, where Broad edged a ball to first slip off Ashton Agar's bowling but did not "walk". Umpire Aleem Dar did not signal out but replays showed Broad edged the ball that was caught, and he should have been on his way. Broad at that point had scored 37 runs and went on to make 65. England won the Test by 14.

Broad later said he regretted saying the remarks to Cummins.

Cummins summed up the situation simply: "For what I think is a pretty common non-event, it does seem like everyone has a pretty strong opinion about it. I don't think there's any discussion; it's out. If the shoe was on the other foot, I wouldn't be looking at the opposition, I'd probably be thinking about our own batter, and would be thinking it's pretty silly.

"I don't think a conversation about the spirit of cricket even comes into a dismissal like that. It was plain and simple a stumping."

Former England captains Michael Atheron and Andrew Strauss both described Bairstow's casual stroll out of his crease as "dozy".

What was Bairstow thinking when he wandered off with the ball thudding into Carey's gloves?

The Australians had already noted he was prone to doing a Deon and the Belmonts ("The Wanderer").

Cummins, in the Prime Video documentary *The Test - Season Three*, said he noticed Bairstow walking out of his crease repeatedly during the Lord's Test.

"I saw him do it a couple of balls in a row," Cummins said.

He revealed he told wicketkeeper Carey to have a shot at the stumps: "So I just said to Kez (Carey) just have a throw."

Cummins said he had never concealed his involvement and to be fair, he was probably never asked about it. He did say he felt sorry for Carey who bore the brunt of the abuse and criticism.

Cummins remained certain there was nothing wrong with the dismissal. In after-match interviews, he pointed out that Bairstow had rolled the ball at the stumps in not dissimilar circumstances during the same match.

"You see Jonny do it all the time, he did it day one to Warner, he did it in 2019 to Steve (Smith), it's a really common thing for keepers to do," Cummins said.

"There was no pause, he (Carey) catches it and throws it straight at the stumps. I thought it was totally fair play. That's the rule. Some people might disagree but…the rule is there and that is the way I saw it."

Social media backed up Cummins, footage posted showing Bairstow trying the same action against Marnus Labuschagne just two days previously.

The fount of all cricket knowledge, Wisden, noted:

"Bairstow comfortably ducked under the last delivery of Green's over with the ball travelling safely through to Carey behind the stumps. Immediately after collecting the ball, Carey threw the ball at the stumps. Bairstow, unaware of what was going on behind him, had strolled out of his crease, leaving the crease before the ball dislodged the bails. The decision was checked upstairs by the TV umpire Marais Erasmus but replays confirmed that Bairstow was well out of his ground. While the Lord's crowd voiced their displeasure at the dismissal, it is uncontroversial according to the game's Laws.

"Law 20 concerns when a ball becomes dead and states that a ball is dead when it is 'finally settled', which is 'is a matter for the umpire alone to decide.' The standing umpire Ahsan Raza had not called over. On the Sky Sports Cricket commentary, Mike Atherton relayed a message from former award-winning umpire Simon Taufel who said that a ball is still live until 'both sides disregard that the ball is in play'.

IT'S JUST NOT CRICKET

As Carey threw the ball as soon as he collected the ball, it was clear that Australia regarded the ball in play."

Carey explained how events unfolded when the Australians saw Bairstow ducking under Cameron Green bouncers: "We were switched on to the fact that it was a bouncer plan and it felt like Jonny was…getting out of the way, he wasn't playing any shots.

"When he ducked, obviously his first movement was pretty much out of his crease so instinctively I grabbed the ball, threw the stumps down and the rest is history. He's a fantastic player and obviously a big wicket in that match."

Carey copped a pasting from several quarters.

In the "The Test" documentary, Usman Khawaja said everyone was singling out Kez (Carey); "I just feel so bad for him what he went through at the time and what his family would have gone through being there at the time. It would have been so hard."

Khawaja revealed Bairstow had tried to do the same thing to him and Warner earlier in the series.

England coach New Zealander Brendon McCullum was furious with the Australians and said England could skip post-series beers with them.

"I can't imagine we'll be having a beer with them any time soon," McCullum said after the match.

English newspapers raged, some even demanding an apology from Australia.

English TV shock jock Piers Morgan used his social media platform to lambast the Australians.

"If there's one thing worse than Australia so brazenly abusing the spirit of cricket, it's seeing the miscreants now chortling away about it," Morgan said.

Spirit of cricket? Bodyline?

England captain Ben Stokes claimed later he would have withdrawn the appeal had he been in Australia's shoes, arguing that Bairstow had thought the ball was dead and it was over. Only thought?

"I'm a person who really likes to stay within his own space," Stokes said. "I asked a few questions out there (to the umpires) when the whole thing went on, but I chose not to engage myself any further. I didn't want to get myself side-tracked.

"I am not disputing the fact it is out because it is out. Would I want to win a game in that manner? The answer for me is no."

The Bairstow incident fell short of becoming a full-blown international incident beyond cricket, although the Prime Ministers of both countries had their say.

A spokesman for UK Prime Minister Rishi Sunak said: "The Prime Minister agrees with Ben Stokes. He said he simply wouldn't want to win a game in the manner Australia did."

Australia's Prime Minister Anthony Albanese sided with his country's Test team: "I'll remind him (Sunak) that...when I was at primary school teachers taught me as they teach every Australian youngster – keep your bat in your crease, stay in your crease."

Cummins pointed out the decision to send Bairstow on his way rested with the umpires. Simply, Bairstow left his crease before "over" was called.

Alex Carey later told how he was dismissed in a similar fashion to Bairstow when he was 15, playing his first match for Glenelg's A-grade team in Adelaide Premier Cricket.

He had complained to his captain, former South Australia batsman Ben Hook, who had little sympathy and told the young Carey: "You'll remember to keep your foot behind the line next time."

Questions about the "spirit of the game" remained long after the Lord's Test.

McCullum was reminded that he had in his playing career twice run out batters as they were celebrating milestone innings. Sri Lankan's Murali Muralitharan had been one of McCullum's run-out victims when he left the crease to celebrate a batting partner's century. McCullum some time later apologised.

Hardly a cricket match is completed without controversy. Even the use of modern technology hasn't eased debate about whether a batter has been out caught cleanly (even nicked at all) or out LBW to a ball that is deemed to have been hitting the stumps. Repeated replays of such incidents serve only to add to questions about decisions.

Before the use of technology, controversies often arose over decisions such as handling the ball, obstructing fielders, hit-wicket and catches.

These days, television replays are most effective in determining run-outs and stumpings (even no-balls) that were too close to call for an umpire relying on his own vision. Suspicions remain about the accuracy of such things as ball-tracking and Snicko.

• • •

When it comes to dodgy run-outs and injustices, cricket aficionados may want to point to an act by the English team in Australia more than 125 years previously, when there was no technology to adjudicate and even greater weight was given to "the spirit of the game," more so than seems to be the case now.

In 1897, two brothers, – Bob and Charlie Mcleod – were playing for Victoria and Australia. Charlie gained prominence, albeit in controversial circumstances.

According to cricket historian Abhishek Mukherjee, "Charles Edward McLeod was one of the best all-rounders of the Golden Age of Cricket. A Victorian turn-of-the-century all-rounder, McLeod was a more-than-adept medium-paced bowler who had picked up 335 wickets at 24.25; he was also a dependable batsman who had scored 3,321 runs at 21.28."

This record earned him a Test call-up.

If you thought the under-arm bowling incident in New Zealand was a bit ordinary, then what happened to Charlie was at least equally as controversial.

Charlie was deaf, yet managed to play 16 Tests for Australia.

In the first Test of the 1897 series against England, at the SCG on 16 December, England batted first and were bowled out for 551 on the second afternoon. McLeod and Ernie Jones each took three wickets. John Kelly became the first wicket-keeper to have not conceded a single bye in an innings of over 500 runs (has that ever been repeated?).

At 5 for 82 in reply, McLeod joined Hugh Trumble at the wicket.

Wickets fell quickly, leaving McLeod stranded on 50 with Australia bowled out for 237.

Asked to follow-on, McLeod was promoted to number three. He and Joe Darling added 89 before stumps. Darling was on 80 and McLeod 20, Australia finishing the day 1-126, but still 188 runs short of England's total.

Early next morning. Australia added nine more runs with McLeod contributing six of them when drama unfolded.

Abhishek Mukherjee takes up the story:

"Richardson bowled a full-toss to McLeod; the Victorian missed the line completely and the ball hit the stumps. The Englishmen were jubilant at having broken the partnership, but Charles Bannerman, umpiring in the match, had already called 'no-ball' rather loudly.

"Unfortunately, McLeod's handicap (he was deaf, remember) prevented him from hearing the call; he walked out of the crease on his way to the pavilion. The ball had rolled to Bill Storer behind the stumps; Storer threw down the stumps with McLeod out of the crease. Jim Philips, standing at square-leg, had no option but to rule McLeod run out.

IT'S JUST NOT CRICKET

"McLeod was confused at first before getting to terms with exactly what had happened. Once he realised that the Englishmen had been cruel enough to take advantage of his handicap he appealed to Bannerman as a last resort; Bannerman, however, refused to intervene.

"McLeod returned to the pavilion amidst a lot of hooting and jeering from the crowd; the afternoon was spent in discussion on whether the run out was a legitimate one given that McLeod had not exactly attempted a run. Storer, on the other hand, 'regretted at having acted as he did, and said he did so under orders'."

Australia won all four Tests after the runout incident. McLeod, a right-handed batsman and medium-pace bowler, finished the series with 352 runs at 58.67 and 10 wickets at 23.60 from five Tests. His career after that tapered. In the other 12 Tests he played he managed only 221 runs at 12.28 and 23 wickets at 47.35.

He scored a total of 573 Test runs (av 23.87) and 3321 first-class runs (av 21.28). He took 33 Test wickets (at 40.15) and 335 first-class wickets (at 24.25).

Charlie McLeod died at Armadale, Victoria, on 26 November 1918.

• • •

In all the discussions that raged in the mainstream media and what passes for social media these days, there was little mention of bodyline, probably the greatest controversy still to afflict the game's "spirit."

On 16 January 1933, Australian batsman Bert Oldfield collapsed on the Adelaide wicket, his skull fractured by a lightning-bolt delivery from Harold Larwood.

The tactic employed by England under the captain, Douglas Jardine, was for a right-arm fast bowler to go around-the-wicket, and into the body of the right-handed batter. The short-pitched delivery (landing outside the line of leg stump and angling in) would intimidate the batter and he'd fend the ball off to an array of leg-side fielders.

The reason? As England arrived in Australia, Don Bradman was averaging 139.4. Simply, he was too good for the England bowlers. The answer? Attack the batter rather than the stumps.

Larwood had the ideal weapon for the tactic – deliveries that supposedly could touch on 100 mph (160 km/h in the metric era). Bowl fast, high-bouncing deliveries towards the leg stump of the wicket – where a batsman would usually stand.

A batter had few viable choices – get hit or get out.

The 50,000 people at the Adelaide ground that day let the English know their feelings in no uncertain terms. It was later reported some of the English players were in fear of their lives as the crowed bellowed.

Wisden would later call it "probably the most unpleasant Test ever played."

MCC tour manager Pelham Warner, seeking to smooth relationships, was sent packing by Australian captain Bill Woodfull with what were, for some years, the 25 most famous words in sport: "I don't want to see you, Mr Warner. There are two teams out there. One is trying to play cricket and the other is not."

There were exchanges between governments, threats of boycotts and the ill-feeling lasted for years.

Eventually, rules were introduced to outlaw the leg-side tactic and even later, fielding restrictions were introduced to render persistent leg-side bowling virtually useless and punishable on the scoreboard.

There were repercussions for some of the players. Jardine retired the next year and Larwood never played for England again.

Encouraged by some foes from the Bodyline series, Larwood emigrated to Australia in 1950 and became friends with Bert Oldfield. He was awarded an MBE in 1993, aged 88. He died on 22 July 1995.

Though bodyline is effectively outlawed, the short-pitched ball is still used to this day to intimidate batters, almost all of whom wear helmets and face-protection when facing pace bowlers.

The standard of protective gear is always under review and has been since November 2014, when Australian Test batsman Phillip Hughes, 25, died after being struck on the top of the neck by a ball during a domestic match in Sydney. Hughes had been wearing a helmet, but a short-pitched ball evaded the guard.

The fourth day of the Ashes second Test at Lord's in July 2023 saw the "quicks" from both sides dropping the ball short to counter the slowness off the pitch – Cummins and Starc for Australia and England captain Ben Stokes putting Bazball aside, spread the field and with the bowlers pitching short.

Australia lost 8-92 in 40 overs after the short-ball assault started, with all eight dismissals coming from bouncers.

According to Sky Sports, 98 per cent of deliveries during the afternoon session of the fourth day were "short balls". According to *CricViz*, only 10 deliveries landed on a good length or fuller in the entire session.

Australia won the Test by 43 runs.

Cummins' view of short-pitched bowling: "It's a delicate balance sometimes," he told *ESPNCricinfo* in October 2023, "where you're trying to keep the run rate in check, try and go for three or four or an over, or do you try and risk it to pick up those vital wickets?"

• • •

Jonny Bairstow's ability to get out in unusual circumstances didn't end at Lord's in 2023.

He was run out after a deflection off Ishant Sharma's right hand, caught out of his crease at the non-striker's end in his first match of the 2024 IPL, playing for Punjab Kings against Delhi Capitals.

Batsman Prabhsimran Singh charged at a slower ball by Ishant. Prabhsimran, surprised that it was a slower ball, checked his shot and played the ball along the ground towards the stumps at the non-striker's end. Ishant stuck his hand out as he fell to the ground. The ball rolled on to the stumps, with Bairstow in a desperate dive to try to regain his ground.

Ishant appealed, indicating he touched the ball before it hit the stumps. The television replay showed Ishant had got a finger on the ball, and that Bairstow was just centimetres short of his ground. He was out for nine runs from just three balls.

• • •

Discussion of controversial stumpings and runouts inevitably turns to the Mankad incident.

Run-out or stumping the batter at the non-striker's end as a ball is about to be bowled has become an issue in modern cricket, particularly in short forms of the game where every advantage is sought to get every run or wicket that's so vital to securing a result.

The chance to get such a dismissal is more likely when a slow bowler is operating and the non-striker is backing up.

The Mankad owes its name to Indian cricketer Vinoo Mankad who ran out Bill Brown in the Test match between Australian and India in Sydney in the 1947-48 series. Brown was caught backing up out of his crease as Mankad ran in to bowl. Instead of letting the ball go, Mankad flicked off the bails.

The Mankad is rarely seen in Test cricket any more.

It has been recorded just four times in Tests, starting with Mankad. Charlie Griffith did it to Ian Redpath when the West Indies played Australia in Adelaide in 1968-69 and Ewen Chatfield did it to Derek Randall when New Zealand played England in Christchurch in 1977-78.

The last time it was seen in a Test was in Perth in the 1978-79 series when Australia played Pakistan. The bowler was paceman Alan Hurst and the batter was Sikander Bakht. It was the last wicket to fall in Pakistan's second innings with Hurst having taken nine wickets for the match.

There was another controversial incident in that match. Australian opener Andrew Hilditch was given out "handled the ball" in Australia's second innings. Hilditch picked up a wayward throw from the outfield and returned the ball to bowler Sarfaraz Nawaz, who appealed immediately.

Australia won the Test by seven wickets.

As for the Mankad these days, bowlers are more likely to warn the batter about leaving the crease too early rather than effect a dismissal, even though the rules of the game would allow it.

Cummins was asked about whether he would ever consider "Mankad-ing" a batter.

His answer was simple: "It's a waste of energy." He added: "When I'm running in, I don't see the batters at all. I think Josh Hazlewood (fellow Australian fast bowler) said… 'It's way too far to run in to give a warning or to attempt a run out'."

He was asked in 2022 if bowlers were losing their patience with batters who left their crease at the bowling end too early, particularly in the short forms of the game.

"It's a weird time in that I think it's transitioning from something that was maybe frowned upon to something that is considered just a run out," he said. "So, I think it's just those reminders to kind of show that you do have the power to pull the trigger if you want to. I'm not sure every bowler will, but instead warn the batsman that they've got to be careful."

AUTHOR'S NOTE: As far as I am aware I am not directly related to Bob and Charlie though clearly our heritage goes back to the Macleod Clan.

14

A VIEW FROM THE OUTER

Whether Pat Cummins ends his Test cricket career as Australia's best ever captain or even best ever fast bowler remains to be seen.

He has probably another five years of Test cricket left and may well achieve the level of success of which he seems capable – in both endeavours.

I have seen quite a lot of cricket, mostly on television. Test cricket usually only comes to Melbourne for the annual Boxing Day Test at the Melbourne Cricket Ground.

What I most remember is the Australian bowling attack of Thomson and Lillee. Len Pascoe could also be troublesome alongside them with his great pace, too. The record of Cummins at the G may not have attracted the hero worship afforded the aforementioned, but a 10-wicket haul in a Boxing Day Test is something to be celebrated.

Cummins in December 2023 against Pakistan became the 10th Australian to take 250 Test wickets. His "stats" placed him at the best to do so at the time– an average of 22.32 and a strike rate of 46.70, the only one with an average under 23 and a strike rate under 48.

The MCG has several "local" heroes, mostly fast bowlers who seemed to find an extra gear when they ran in, spurred on by the roars of large and quite partisan crowds. Lillee, Thomson and Pascoe were devastating.

A true local hero though was Max "Tangles" Walker. The MCG was his territory.

Max had also played VFL (now AFL) football at senior level for Melbourne, the team that recruited him from Tasmania in 1966. He switched to cricket in 1967.

Why "Tangles"?

His bowling action was, to put it politely, unique – bowling right arm over his right leg. His nickname began as "Tanglefoot" but became "Tangles". If golf commentator David Feherty likened watching Phil Mickelson playing golf to "watching a drunk chasing a balloon near the edge of a cliff," what would he have made of Tangles?

His action was instantly recognisable.

Walker turned out to have a comedic bent, as well. He put his name to 14 books over more than 20 years. One I remember best is "How to Hypnotise Chooks and other great yarns." Not Pulitzer prizeworthy, but easy to ready and a good laugh.

The larrikin Max became the face of an advertising campaign for Aerogard insect repellent. Anything at all bother you?" a youngster asks Max. "Batsmen and flies."

"Have a good weekend Mr Walker" became a catch-phrase.

Max Walker retired from cricket mid-way through the 1981-82 season. Books and public speaking became is forte.

When he was bowling at the MCG, he always had the crowd on his side.

He wasn't bad at bowling either, although I understand when his cricket career began in Tasmania he was a budding opening batter.

He switched from football to cricket, also for Melbourne, as an opening bowler.

He went on to play for Victoria, then Australia. He played 34 Test matches, taking 138 wickets, his best being 8-143 against England at the MCG in 1975. He scored 586 runs at an average of 19.53.

Max was 68 when he died but he left cricket fans with a lot of fond memories.

Walker is just a raft of players who made their names at the MCG, even though he was often first-change after Lillee and Thomson. He also joined World Series cricket for two years, the song "C'mon Assie, C'mon" announcing " Mr Walker's playing havoc with the bats."

He was a legend.

Bowlers seemed to hog the limelight in MCG Tests. The highest wicket takers have been Dennis Lillee (82), Shane Warne (76), Hugh Trumble (46), Graham McKenzie (45) and Glenn McGrath (42).

I didn't see anything of Trumble and only little of Graham (Garth) McKenzie.

Nathan Lyon heads the list of active champions of the MCG with 50 wickets. Test skipper Pat Cummins boosted his tally with the 10-wicket haul against Pakistan in the 2023 Boxing Day Test.

By mid-2024 his Test tally was 269 wickets. Fans look forward to seeing that grow, particularly now that a five-Tests series has been reinstated against India, for November-January 2024-25.

• • •

Cricket fans have their favourite batters. Starting with the all-time greats, Don Bradman heads the list.

He had one of the best performances of his career in the 1936-37 Ashes series at the MCG, scoring 270 runs from 275 balls. He scored his first century in Test cricket at the MCG on 29 December 1928. He went on to score 1,671 runs there in his career, 1928-48.

I didn't see Bradman first-hand, only segments of flickering film. He is best remembered for finishing his Test career with an average of 99.9, something we will most likely never see again. He was out for a duck in his last innings.

I did see the great I.V.A. Richards get a century at the MCG one day when an injured leg meant he could hardly run – see the ball, hit it to the boundary.

As you would expect the best batting figures at the G belong to Australians.

A VIEW FROM THE OUTER

After Bradman, Ricky Ponting scored 1,338, Steve Waugh 1,284 and Allan Border 1,272.

Interesting that the top four were all captains.

One Australian Test cricketer who seems to be forgotten sometimes in discussions about the "best" is Doug Walters.

Doug Walters AM MBE was inducted into the Sport Australia Hall of Fame in 1994 as an Athlete Member for his contribution to the sport of cricket.

His contribution: He scored 5,357 Test runs at an average of 48.26 including 15 centuries. He took 49 Test wickets at an average of 29.08. Close to being a genuine Test all-rounder.

"Dungog Doug" as he became known, after his home town in NSW, had an enviable junior record as a bowler – returns of 9-8, 9-4 and 8-7 playing for the Police Boys Club.

He burst on to the representative cricket scene as a batter, called in as a late replacement in a NSW Colts XI team against Queensland, batting at No. 7 and making 140 runs not out.

It was all up from there, graduating to the NSW team as a 17-year-old where one of the first bowlers he had to face was West Indian great Wes Hall who was playing for Queensland. Walters made 50 in the second innings.

Just before his 20th birthday, he made 155 on his Test debut in Brisbane against England. After that he seemed to reel off century after century, and didn't appear at all menaced by the fearsome West Indies pace attack, either in Australia or in the West Indies.

I heard from afar when he entered the record books with a Test century in a session. He averaged 71 against West Indies in 1972/73. His score of 112 at Port of Spain in 148 minutes included 100 between lunch and tea. Wisden noted: "By any standards it was a magnificent innings."

Walters three times scored 100 in a session.

He missed two years of cricket, conscripted to do national service in the Vietnam War call-up. He returned to the Test arena in 1968 where he averaged 127 in two Tests that year against the touring Indians.

Ian Chappell: "Walters was the best player of off-spin bowling I have seen; he didn't just survive against the very best, he occasionally battered them into submission. He scored a sublime hundred on a Madras mine-field in facing the off-spin wizardry of Erapalli Prasanna."

Chappell concluded: "Walters was a freak, who, though he often stayed up late drinking and smoking, could still perform at the highest level."

Perhaps not the ideal role-model in this day and age, but he was a hero back then.

• • •

Ian Chappell was captain of Australia for 30 Test matches, so how does he rate in the skippers of the modern era?

He first led Australia in the 1970-71 Test series against England taking over the captaincy from Bill Lawry for the final Test in that series and resigned after the 1975 series against England. He led in 30 Tests for 15 wins, 10 draws and five losses.

Lawry became the first captain to be dropped mid-series, heavily criticised for being too defensive. He was 33 years old and had averaged 47.15, mostly as a solid opener. He switched to commentary where he was hit with audiences with catch-phrases such as "Got him" and "It's all happening here." Many listeners learnt quite a bit about pigeon racing (his hobby) from Lawry's commentary.

Allan Border was Australia's longest serving captain, for 90 Test matches. Draws outnumbered victories, 38-32, with 22 losses (one tie).

Ricky Ponting was captain for 77 Tests for 48 wins, 16 losses and 13 draws.

Steve Waugh boasts the best record as captain in the modern era (20th Century onwards) with a win record of 71.92% from 57 matches in charge.

I rate him ahead of Mark Taylor, Michael Clarke (nominated by Ian Chappell as the best), Steve Smith (the best batting average) and

Tim Paine. Smith's captaincy took a big black mark in the "sandpaper-gate" scandal of March 2018 on his watch when leadership should have come to the fore.

Waugh may not have had the batting elegance of his brother Mark, or Greg Chappell, but his batting average of 51.06 showed he could "walk the talk."

He led the Australian Test cricket team from 1999 to 2004 and was the most capped Test cricket player in history, with 168 appearances, until India's Sachin Tendulkar broke the record in 2010.

S. Waugh (nicknamed Tugga) was gritty with the bat, and ball, something that was evident when as he set out on his cricket career with Bankstown in Sydney and later highlighted when at the Gabba in 1988 the 23-year-old all-rounder had the audacity to bowl bouncers at West Indies legend Viv Richards.

He showed a bit of "mongrel" in Brisbane after his team had faced a barrage of short-pitched bowling. So, he had a dip himself, pitching three successive short balls that passed over the great man's head.

I remember him explaining what was going through his mind at the time. He said he'd been in the Test team for a couple of years and believed his place was in doubt, having got out "meekly" to some shorter balls.

He had to up the ante. He was sick of losing to the then-powerhouse West Indies team.

Richards laughed as the first bounced passed safely over his head. The next one got his attention. Not a smile that time, not the third time either.

Waugh had shown the courage that would mark the captaincy he would begin 11 years later.

He was to say that was a turning point in his career, and possibly for the team, too.

He said Richards a couple of years later told him he respected what he'd done.

Comparing captains across eras is not an exact science, as much depends on the players that were available at the time, and as usual the standard of the opposition.

For example, Zimbabwe captain Alistair Campbell lost 57.4 % of matches in which he was captain – unfair to be critical as Zimbabwe was not a powerhouse in world cricket. What is surprising however is to see that David Gower of England lost 56.25% of matches in which he was captain.

According to *Howstat*, the four Test captains of all time with the best winning record are all Australians; Steve Waugh (71.93%), Don Bradman (62.50%), Ricky Ponting (62.34%) and Pat Cummins (60.71%).

These days, Steve Waugh is a motivational leadership speaker. He has had several mentoring roles, including with the Socceroos, Australian Olympic athletes, the Australian Cricket Team and the GWS AFL team in Sydney.

He still supports charities through the Steve Waugh Foundation. The main work is in the area of rare diseases among children.

He has supported the Udayan rehabilitation home for children of leprosy sufferers in India since 1998, in particular raising funds for Nivedita Bhavan, the girls' wing of the facility.

Which brings me back to Pat Cummins. He's still new in captaincy but he shows the same kind of care for his players, people in general and the world as did (and does) Steve Waugh.

More success on the cricket pitch, and Cummins can be promoted to the top of my list of greatest Test captains.

• • •

I remember an interview NSW coach Mick Pawley did for the newspaper I was working on in country NSW.

Pawley spoke about a match between Bankstown and another team in the Sydney Grade competition.

Bankstown had two express bowlers – Jeff Thomson and Len Pascoe (the latter had changed his name from Durtanovich). The pair hadn't made it into the NSW team at that stage but soon would be lining up in the Test team. Pawley related how in one game (against Manly), the two Bankstown speedsters sent a couple of batters to hospital.

In a later interview, Pascoe was asked about the impact he and Thomson had on grade cricket. "It was scary," he said. "We did not know what we were capable of. There was a ward named after us at Bankstown Hospital. It was usually used during home games."

Their combination took beating. Sensibly, Tony Greig chose to wear a crash-helmet when he faced them during the formation of World Series Cricket.

In the modern era, Cummins, Hazlewood and Starc will go into the history books as one of the most lethal combinations of all time. Would anyone dare face them without a helmet and a wad of protection to other parts?

Are they better than Lillee and Thommo (and Pascoe)?

That's one for cricket fans.

• • •

My own cricket experience was one of specialist No.10 or 11 batter who sometimes tried to bowl leg-cutters, something my father had been pretty good at apparently, even taking the new ball occasionally and once taking a hat-trick in an inter-district game. He always claimed one of his hat-trick wickets against Inverell was Rick McCosker's father, but that's all we have to go on.

I took the new ball once, in a B grade game in country NSW on matting over an ant-bed pitch. Our wickets were either mats on ant-bed, malthoid or concrete – spinners had to work hard for their wickets. There was one turf wicket in the district, constructed from Bulli black soil that was also used at the SCG and trucked in specially. The turf wicket made life unpredictable for batters.

I digress. Our opening bowler was late to the game and the opposition had decided to bat, possibly on the strength of the non-appearance of our key young tear-away bowler.

The captain gave me the ball. I don't know whose decision it was, but I was to bowl at a left-hander from around the wicket. Maybe our captain, Earl, knew more about cricket than we sometimes game him credit for. Perhaps the batter got something in his eye, but he missed a ball that wasn't probably even medium pace, even if it was delivered from a long run-up.

He was out, bowled. One more over and I thought it best to retreat to a fielding a position, 1-10 to my name. I managed to win a trophy for catching one year. Again, in the absence of some regulars, I opened the batting twice, managing a 50 and a 35. But that was the career really. No baggy green for me.

• • •

Back in the day, cricket matches between media houses were something to look forward to. When the *Melbourne Herald* played the *Adelaide News*, Ashley Mallett, former Test player was in the Adelaide line-up. When the *Melbourne Herald* played the *Leader* Group in Melbourne, former Test player Simon O'Donnell was in the *Leader* team.

It seems the Herald team, of which I was sometimes a member, always came up against someone better credentialled in the game than most of us.

Our captain in these days was Ron Reed, a sportswriter on *The Herald* and a mighty useful fast bowler. His nickname was Hound, said by some to have come from his liking to keep the ball for long stints at the bowling crease.

Sadly, Reed died suddenly in 2022. At one time he was my boss in the Sports department of the *Melbourne Herald*. He remained a good mate through the years.

Reed was a cricket enthusiast – the perfect choice to write the tribute book *Captain Pat*, about the fast bowler appointed as Australia's cricket captain in 2021, the first fast bowler to get the permanent role.

Little wonder given Reed's reputation in sports journalism that Cummins gave his time for interviews in *Captain Pat*.

On a trip to Sydney to play the News Limited team at a picturesque cricket oval, Randwick, Reed was our captain.

This was an uneventful outing for us but the day became notorious in cricket history for an incident that occurred back home at the MCG where many of us would have been had it not been for the interstate trip.

Many cricket fans probably still haven't forgiven Australia for the underarm bowling incident on 1 February 1981. During an ODI match Australian captain Greg Chappell instructed his brother Trevor (who at one time played for Bankstown) to bowl the final ball of the match underarm so that the batsman on strike, Brian McKechnie, who needed a six to steal victory for the visitors, couldn't loft it out of the ground.

The news filtered through to *The Herald* team sitting on the hill at Randwick.

Our captain, always a man of few, yet poignant, words, said gruffly "He did f......g what".

That incident is still the subject of much debate when Aussies and Kiwis get together socially.

And the same probably will be the case between Poms and Aussies when the topic turns to the runout of Johnny Bairstow in 2023.

• • •

A final tribute to Ron Reed: In a social game he tossed me the ball for an over and retreated to the straight-hit boundary. Was he expecting something in particular?

After three successive full-tosses, there're was that gruff voice from the man with few but poignant words again – "Anything in the wicket?"

15

THE GAP YEARS

Graduating St Paul's Grammar School in Sydney, the 18-year-old Pat Cummins was heading into university studies. But within just a few weeks of his last day at school, he was playing in the elite state-based competition for the NSW cricket team.

University would have to wait.

Cummins already had come to notice as a talented express bowler in his junior days and had state representation under his belt.

He recalled to Ron Reed how he rose through the ranks at whirlwind pace.

He was sitting on a train travelling to university when his phone rang. It was chairman of selectors Andrew Hilditch saying: "Congratulations, you've received a Cricket Australia contract." That was June 2011.

Cummins had only just turned 18.

"I remember sitting on the train, trying not to squeal because there were people sitting around me," he recalled. "I'm thinking, this is wild.

"That CA contract (list) had names like Ricky Ponting, Michael Clarke – legends of the game – and I was now part of that squad of 20-odd people.

"It was my first full-time job. I remember thinking I don't have to catch the train every single day, I can go and buy myself a car. So I bought a second-hand Mazda 3 as a late birthday present."

Hilditch had no reservations about Cummins' young age. "We don't think it's a gamble, we think he's going to be real good," Hilditch had said.

In October, he was in South Africa, part of the Australian squad, albeit in short-form cricket.

Reed: "There, soaking up information and dressing room culture from all the big names around him – and generally having the time of his young life – he made his international debut in a T20, pinching himself because he had played only two professional games for NSW to that point where he had taken zero wickets and gone for about eight an over."

He played two T20I and three ODI matches, (taking 10 wickets, 5 in each series) in South Africa. Next stop was home, and who knows what?

But a surprise was in store for the youngster.

In November 2011, he was called up to the national squad for the two-match Test series that was to follow the short-form games in South Africa. He was to replace young Victorian James Pattinson in the squad that had been in Sri Lanka a month earlier.

"Patrick Cummins has gained selection ahead of James for this tour," chairman of selectors Andrew Hilditch said in a statement.

"Patrick is a very exciting prospect and at just 18 years of age is already showing the ability to have a significant impact at international level.

"Patrick would have most likely been on the tour of Sri Lanka if not for injury at the end of last season.

"Now he's back fit and bowling well, we saw this as the right time to bring him into the Test squad for this important series."

The Australian squad for the Tests was Michael Clarke (c), Shane Watson (vc), Michael Beer, Trent Copeland, Patrick Cummins, Brad Haddin, Ryan Harris, Phil Hughes, Mike Hussey, Mitchell Johnson, Usman Khawaja, Nathan Lyon, Shaun Marsh, Ricky Ponting, Peter Siddle.

Next step for Pat Cummins was a Test debut, something to which he may have aspired but hadn't factored in when he packed his kit to go to South Africa for limited overs cricket.

"The whole world where I thought I was going...turned upside down and it was just a career I never thought I could have," Cummins said later.

"Once I was on the Australian tour I looked around, and everyone in that team had been playing for five, 10, 15 years...I thought; 'How good is this? If I don't stuff up here, you know, hopefully, I can have a similar kind of career'."

Australia was always going to have a difficult time against the home team in the Tests. Since South Africa's 2-0 loss away to Sri Lanka in 2006, the Proteas boasted an intimidating record – they'd won all but one their next 10 series (the one loss against India on the subcontinent).

For Australia, the series was going to be one step on the way to rebuilding after the retirements of Warne, McGrath, Hayden, Langer and Gilchrist. Clarke had only just taken on the captaincy, replacing Ponting who was coming to the end of his career; Australia was in the infancy of Michael Clarke's captaincy and the twilight years of Ricky Ponting's career.

Cummins was in the squad for the Tests but did not make it into the side for the first Test at Newlands from 9-11 November. He was still on a learning curve when he sat in the dressing room to watch Australia's capitulation at Newlands (South Africa won by eight wickets).

Victory was snatched away from the Australians when it seemed to be within their grasp.

Cummins had played all of Australia's five white-ball games before the Tests, finishing as the leading bowler of the series.

That caught the attention of the Test selectors.

A test debut may yet have been a few games away had it not been for injury to Ryan Harris. Australian captain Michael Clarke told Cummins after the first Test that he'd be playing in the second Test at the Wanderers ground in Johannesburg, starting on 17 November.

THE GAP YEARS

Former captain Ricky Ponting presented Cummins with his baggy green on the field at The Wanderers to an enthusiastic greeting from the Australian players and staff.

Australia needed a "rabbit out of the hat" moment.

The magic was to come from tearaway young paceman Pat Cummins, making his Test debut in only his fourth career first-class match. As the record shows, he became Australia's youngest Test cricketer since Ian Craig in 1953, aged 18 years and 193 days.

South Africa named an unchanged line-up, won the toss and elected to bat. Australia made one change, Cummins in for the injured Harris.

As far as a debut in Test cricket match goes, Pat Cummins didn't return spectacular figures when he bowled in the first innings.

Hopefully, viewers didn't adjust their sets – his fireworks were ignited in the second innings.

The debut of Pat Cummins at the Wanderers ground became etched in Australian cricket folklore.

Cummins was quick, that much was certain as the speed gun recorded several balls above 140 km/h in the first innings.

He managed just one wicket that cost 38 runs from 15 overs as South Africa made 266, a total that was likely to be tricky to chase down.

Thanks to openers Usman Khawaja and Phillip Hughes who both made 88, Australia was able to post 296 in reply. Cummins made just two runs, coming in at number 10.

The match was, as they say, on a knife-edge. South Africa set about posting a score in the second innings that would challenge the Australians. Thanks to a century from Hashim Amla, the home team made 339.

But the story of the South African innings wasn't their batting. Pat Cummins sent down 29 overs conceding just 79 runs, and grabbing six wickets in the process, five of them behind the wickets – three batters were caught by keeper Haddin, two were caught by the captain Clarke. One was bowled.

PAT CUMMINS

Incredibly, the speed gun clocked his fastest delivery at 161.1 km/h. (The fastest ever officially recorded was 161.3 km/h credited to Shoaib Akhtar in the 2003 World Cup).

Australia faced a difficult run chase – any total of more than 300 was considered problematic in a second innings by a team chasing victory. The task facing Australia was to score the fourth highest second innings total ever at the Wanderers ground.

All the Australian batters made good starts, Khwaja, Ponting and Haddin the best.

But when they'd gone, it came down to No. 9 Mitchell Johnson. He'd figured in a partnership of 72 with Haddin to create some hope. In the team for his express bowling, Johnson set about the run chase among the tail-enders almost single-handedly once Haddin was out. He was joined by Pat Cummins with the total at 8-292. Only Nathan Lyon was to come.

Cummins went into the match with a total of 27 runs in first-class and limited-overs cricket. As he joined Johnson, Australia still needed 18.

There were some scary moments. A leading edge brought three runs and a few nudges reduced the chase to single figures.

Cummins was riding his luck, but not frightened to "have a go."

He offered a sharp return-catch to Dale Steyn when nine runs were still needed. Steyn put it down and the ball went to the long-off boundary. There was even more drama from that delivery – had the fielder touched the rope? Yes, he had. It was four, leaving five runs to get. Two wickets in hand.

A gate swinging in the wind might have summed up the approach of Cummins for the next few balls.

He survived and Johnson took the next over. He pushed a ball away for a single, leaving Cummins to face the music from spinner Tahir.

Cummins was beaten by a googly that struck him on the pads. Did South Africa get the vital scalp? No, the DRS referral showed he was struck just a centimetre or so outside the line of off-stump. Not out.

Tahir served up a shortish leg-break; the fielders would have seen Cummins' eyes light up as he moved to thrash it through mid-wicket for four. Australia had won.

The tailenders were undefeated, Johnson was 40 not out and Cummins 13 not out.

Cummins earned man of match honours with his 6-79 and scoring the winning runs. He became the second-youngest Test cricketer (behind Enamul Haque Jr of Bangladesh) to take six wickets in an innings.

When the jubilation was over and the dust settled, it was revealed Cummins had carried an injury through his heroics.

He would have it attended to on return to Australia.

The Australians were buoyant – the way ahead looked rosy, with Pat Cummins as the spearhead.

Wicketkeeper Brad Haddin recalled: "He was only a young kid at the time, very raw, very quiet. One thing I noticed, which was different from other kids, he learned very quickly. You only had to tell him once and he soaked it in.

"Patty Cummins at that time was perfect, so raw, hadn't been exposed to all the media. He was just playing cricket. Just playing with his brothers in the backyard."

As the run chase ticked down in that crucial second Test, Haddin recalled: "Nathan Lyon was sitting in the corner dry-retching, as he does, and Pat was just saying, what's wrong, let's just bat, it's just a game of cricket."

Cummins had no compunction in smashing probably the best fast bowler of his era, Dale Steyn, back over his head as he delivered 145 km/h outswingers.

"There's no way I would bat like that now – I was so naïve," Cummins said later.

"It's a funny thing, cricket, you're so nervous waiting to come in to bat or bowl, but once you're in the moment, you're in control so if anything bad happens at least you feel you had some sort of say in it. I guess it's one of the benefits of being 18 years old and fearless."

His bowling effort at Wanderers got the attention of the cricket world, at home and abroad.

Some of his deliveries topped 150 km/h. And he swung the ball both ways, proving to be a real handful.

One commentator noted: "Footage of Cummins ripping out the likes of Jacques Kallis and AB de Villiers was the first they'd seen of the precociously talented youngster."

"There's a lot to work with," Kallis said. "If he stays injury free, he'll have a big career ahead of him."

As it turned out, the "if" was way more significant than anyone imagined at the time. Cricket indeed proved to be a funny game, even tragic.

His injury woes have been well documented. The short story is that Cummins didn't play Test cricket against for just on six years.

First, he missed the 2011-12 summer of Tests through the heel injury he carried through his South African heroics.

He was named in Australia's provisional team for the ICC Under-19 World Cup to be held in Queensland in August 2012 and played for Australia in the 2012 T20 World Cup. He went with the Sydney Sixers to the 2012 Champions League, in South Africa, in October where the Sixers defeated South Africa's Highveld Lions in the final.

Back home in November, he was diagnosed with a stress fracture in his back, ruling him out of the 2012-13 home summer international matches.

He returned in the Australia A team in August 2013, but a recurrence of the stress fracture in his back caused him to miss most of the 2013-14 summer.

How was he going to get back into the form that earmarked him as the spearhead of Australia's bowling attack in the years ahead?

The answer was Dennis Lillee. Cummins would go to Perth to seek the advice of one of Australia's greatest fast bowlers.

When teammate and West Australian Mitch Marsh heard of

THE GAP YEARS

Cummins' plan, he offered the Sydney-sider a bed at his Perth home.

When Cummins turned up he found the bed was in fact a couch. It was no five-star hotel room.

Cummins recalled later: "If I was injured I would go over there and rather than get a hotel room I'd sleep on…well…Mitchy said he had a spare room and I turned up and realised he only had a couch. So he probably gave me more stress fractures, sleeping on his couch!"

Lillee played a significant role in Cummins' rehab and injury from that most recent setback.

The former Australian fast-bowling spearhead, who also endured several injuries during his career, spoke about the role he played.

"I had a lot to do with Pat and his rehab, rearranging and helping him get his action back to something that was protected rather than leaving him open for the injuries that occurred early in his career, very early in his career, put him out for four years or so," Lillee said.

Were there fears that Cummins couldn't come back?

"He was sensational in his first Test match, and you don't lose the talent so I had no doubts at all, and he didn't seem to have any either," Lillee said.

Lillee's experience and understanding of the challenges faced by fast bowlers helped Cummins stay motivated and focused on recovery.

"We spent a lot of time together and he responded and worked bloody hard and you can see the results. When you're that good at 18 you're never going to lose it, it doesn't matter if you get injured," Lillee said.

Lillee worked closely with Cummins on his bowling technique, emphasising the importance of maintaining a balanced action, strengthening core muscles, and avoiding over-exertion.

He taught Cummins how to recognise early signs of fatigue or strain.

Cummins undertook fitness routines to build strength and endurance without risking further injury.

It was mostly about avoiding any further stress fractures. He'd had enough of them.

Lillee encouraged him to stay positive, in challenging times. Cummins credited Lillee's mentoring for shaping his mental toughness.

Cummins resumed in the 2014 BBL after working with Lillee.

When he returned to elite cricket, Cricket Australia was careful to manage him without putting him under too much stress.

He confined his cricket to the white-ball game in 2014 and was picked in the Australian squad for the successful 2015 World Cup campaign. He played in four matches.

Cummins got a late call into the 2015 Ashes squad when Ryan Harris retired, but he did not play in a Test. He played in the ODI and T20I series in the same tour.

During the ODI part of the tour his stress fracture recurred, and he was ruled out of an entire home summer for the fourth time in five years. More intensive rehab followed.

Cummins made his return to domestic cricket in 2016, playing in the NSW one-day squad and the Sydney Thunder Big Bash team. He managed 25 matches in just over four months and seemed to have put his injury woes behind him.

His comeback became complete on 7 March 2017 when he played in the Sheffield Shield for the first time in six years. He bowled 36 overs and claimed eight wickets.

As luck (bad in the case of Starc) would have it, NSW teammate Mitchell Starc was ruled out of the third Test of the Border-Gavaskar Trophy series and was replaced by Cummins.

After five years, three months and 27 days of absence from top-level cricket through injury, Cummins was back playing Test cricket, on 16 March 2017.

He bowled 79 overs in the final two Test matches against India.

Cummins wrote of his frustrations, and fears for his future, in an article for *Athlete's Voice*.

"I had six months of bowling in the nets. I went on a couple of

THE GAP YEARS

Australia A tours. And then I got injured again," he recalled.

"Previously, I'd been injured after playing in a couple of big tournaments. You can cop that. But this time I really hadn't played much. I thought, 'the last four years I've been out injured more than I've been fit. What's to stop this happening again?'

"With every series, every season you miss, there are so many other guys stepping up and playing well.

"You see this long path ahead of you – I first have to run, then I have to bowl off a few steps, then build up and all this is before I even thinking about playing a game and hitting form. Whenever I got caught up thinking about the future, that's when the alarms would start ringing in my head."

During his down time, Cummins took on a university course.

"I'm grateful I had university to focus on," he said. "Studying a business degree at UTS (University of Technology Sydney) gave me some structure and a realisation that life doesn't have to revolve around the cricket calendar. I would have an assignment that I needed to work on and exams I needed to prep for."

That took his mind off his frustrating run of injuries, at least for some of the time. He studied at UTS under its elite athlete program and graduated with his Bachelor of Business degree in 2017. The course he seemed destined to start until cricket intervened was eventually done, thanks to an unwanted break from the game.

Since his return he'd played in 33 of a possible 35 matches to 2024.

Free of injury, cricket had become his business again.

An interviewer once asked Cummins about the players who influenced him in those early years.

"In the early 2000s, when I started watching, the Aussie cricket team was amazing," he said. "Steve Waugh was the captain, and the team was full of greats. Then came Ricky Ponting; I played a little bit with Ricky, but Michael Clarke was my first captain. But, not just the captain, the senior guys.

"When I first started playing, I learnt so much from guys like Shane

Watson, Mike Hussey, Brad Haddin. These are legends of Australian cricket, and I felt really welcomed by those guys when I first walked into the change room."

16

COMETH THE MAN

Pat Cummins had a tough time during the tour of India in 2023, not just on the cricket pitches.

His mother, Maria, was in palliative care with breast cancer and was deteriorating. He left mid-Test to be with his family. Maria died overnight on March 9.

Cummins made it home in time to see and talk to his mother and spent time with family after the funeral.

"It's been good to be home and spend some precious time with family and Mum. And yeah, had a really good send-off for her last week," Cummins told *Fox Sports News* presenter Jim Callinan.

He had known the situation wasn't good when he left the tour after the first two Tests. His mother wasn't well when he started the tour.

"I think the actual playing part was the easiest part," he said.

"You're busy doing something that you love. Knowing that Mum and Dad were back home watching when I was playing so yeah kind of manageable, but I think it was pretty clear that I needed to get home and be with family.

"Once I got home was back being a normal kind of family member and son rather than the other job."

Maria was first diagnosed with breast cancer in 2005 and was a big supporter of the Jane McGrath Foundation.

She died surrounded by her family, including sons Pat, Matt and Tim, and daughters Laura and Kara.

Cummins at one point was expected back in India in time for the final Tests, but he opted to remain home to prepare for the tour of England that would include the World Test Championship final against India before the Ashes. His right place was with his family at that time.

Cummins said he was never mentally present for the Test tour of India; it was the "hardest time of my life" as he grappled with his mother's loss of health.

"I knew when I was getting on that plane (to India) I was going to have to come back in a couple of weeks," he told the ABC.

"Maybe only a handful of people knew that was going to be the case."

The 30-year-old said while he left for India with his parents' best wishes, he did not feel present.

"For those couple of weeks I was in India, especially now I look back at it, my mind was not in India. It was back home the whole time," he said.

"Flying away... that's the hardest time of my life, easily.

"I probably felt, the 12 months leading in, any time I flew away, I was like, 'Time is finite here. I'm making a deliberate choice to go and play somewhere rather than spend it at home'."

Cummins said both COVID-19, when travelling athletes were confined to hotel rooms to maintain their sporting commitments, and the loss of his mother changed his approach to cricket.

"If we're going to be away from our families, let's make sure we're having the time of our lives," he said.

"Play really good cricket, but... pack your golf clubs, bring your coffee machine. If we're in London, go and explore, go and see a show.

"We're trying to create as much space in the diary for people to be able to live their lives.

"It's definitely a lesson learned from Mum. I don't want to waste any time."

The Australians wore black armbands in respect for their captain and Maria for the final Test in Ahmedabad.

The caring side of Pat Cummins can easily be overlooked as he steams in, as the saying goes, from 20 to 22 metres and lets the ball fly at almost 150 km/h towards the batter at the other end of the pitch.

But he is always thinking about his players, too, as he showed at the final Ashes Test, in Hobart in 2023.

Cummins' respect for his teammates – for pretty much everyone, really – was amply demonstrated by an incident immediately after the end of the Hobart Test.

As he and the team gathered on the podium for the customary celebration, spraying champagne over themselves and anybody within reach, Usman Khawaja ducked away.

The Pakistani-born batsman, the first Muslim to play for Australia, wanted to avoid being doused with the alcohol, in accordance with his religious beliefs.

Cummins realised immediately what was happening and shut down the fizz and made sure Khawaja re-joined the celebration.

A small thing? Maybe not in the greater scheme of things after two previous captains had been involved in damaging scandals, but nonetheless an important act of thoughtfulness.

For the Muslim community it was a poignant moment that attracted wide attention. "Every Muslim notices that stuff," said Rana Hussain, Cricket Australia's Diversity and Inclusion manager.

"At the end of big games you watch the Muslim players, 'what are they going to do, how are they going to feel?' and you relate so hard. I did see Usman running away and I thought, oh God, then I saw that they put the bottles away and Pat called him over and was insistent about it. I had a big smile on my face because I thought, 'OK, this is perfect.' There's a time when the sentiment would have been 'alright, well, you don't have to, you've got to miss out' and Pat clocked it – that in itself as amazing. As a Muslim myself it made me smile."

The social media response had been heart-warming, she said.

Khawaja had often spoken about how he had struggled as a young man to fit into the beer-drinking culture of Australian cricket dressing rooms.

The following day he posted the video of the incident with the comment: "If this doesn't show that my teammates have my back, what will? They stopped their celebrations and champagnes so I could join back in. Inclusivity in our game and our values as a sport are so important. I feel like we are trending in the right direction."

Go back even further to 2017 when Cummins was taking tentative steps back into the Australian squad.

He had returned to top-level cricket via limited overs matches after his six years on the sidelines.

What about red-ball cricket?

Cummins reappeared on cricket team sheets for the first time in the long-form game on 7 March 2017, down to play for NSW in the Sheffield Shield competition.

It was home-turf match against South Australia.

Cummins bowled 36 overs in the match, claiming 8-104 as NSW won comfortably.

The plan by medical staff was to use him sparingly, even though he was recalled to the Test squad on 11 March for the tour of India to replace the injured Mitchell Starc.

He played in the third and fourth Test matches of the tour, bowling 79 overs in two weeks. Suffering no ill-effects, he then played in the Indian Premier League.

Cricket fans were eagerly waiting to see what he could achieve back on the world stage as an attack-weapon in the Australian side.

But Cummins had not forgotten his roots forged in cricket at Penrith at the foothills of the Blue Mountains that had been his home growing up.

Penrith were in the final of the Sydney first grade limited overs competition. Cummins was playing for his old side. He probably didn't have to be there, but such were his feelings for his old club where he'd played since he was a teenager, he wanted to be part of the action.

You can imagine the feelings amongst the Hawkesbury players. They were young and playing in their first final in any level of grade cricket. And they would be facing Pat Cummins, hero of the South African tour in 2011 on the comeback trail.

One of Hawkesbury's stars through the season had been former Pakistan under-19s player Aamir Jamal, a player who could shine with bat and ball. Could he counter the Cummins effect?

The game was on a knife-edge. Hawkesbury had been gallant. Penrith had not won a trophy at this level since 2001-02.

Cummins had already claimed three of Hawkesbury's top-order batsmen and he'd bowl what in all likelihood would be the deciding over.

He began with Hawkesbury needing five runs. Penrith needed just one wicket.

Down to the last ball and Hawkesbury need three to win. Penrith still needed that last wicket.

The loud home crowd was behind the local speedster as he roared in. The batter pushed the ball out to deep point. The Hawkesbury men ran the first and turned for the second that would tie the game.

The ball somehow arrived back in the gloves of keeper Tim Cummins, Pat's older brother. The bails were whipped off and Penrith had won.

Club president Paul Goldsmith told the local newspaper: "In the sheds afterwards, Pat was happy as anyone. He really cares about this club. Everyone ran on to the field and that showed how much it meant."

The victory turned into a big party and the club's fridge was quickly emptied. Cummins proffered his credit card to keep the party going. He still cared about his cricketing roots.

Cummins' concern for his fellow humans, extends beyond cricket, well beyond his teammates and the matches in which he plays.

UNICEF, among other organisations, could hardly believe its luck when he came on board. Australian chief of the organisation Tony Stuart said Cummins, who first approached the UN agency during the second Covid wave that swept through India while he was playing there, was no ordinary celebrity sportsman.

Young, principled and willing to offer his own time and money to support the causes he cares about, he was widely seen as representative of a new generation of leader for a sporting public fatigued with scandal, Melbourne's *Herald Sun* reported.

"In times of crisis you see what drives people, and during covid when some people were complaining about quarantines and this and that, Pat reached out to us and wanted to know what he could do to help because he knew first-hand what was happening with Covid in India with families and children," Stuart told the paper.

Cummins' authenticity and generosity – including an initial $50,000 for aid in India and further financial support for early childhood education for indigenous children in Australia – stood out, he said.

"He is so authentic, so caring, so interested in the betterment of children, globally and in Australia. And unlike some sports celebrities who delegated to their agents, Pat genuinely got involved himself," Stuart said.

During his season at SRH in the IPL, Cummins didn't spend his down-time off lazing. He was out in communities doing his bit to make lives a little more pleasurable for the locals, particularly children.

A social media video circulated of him playing cricket with children from a government school in Hyderabad.

His interaction with the children would be memories they could carry for the rest of their lives.

Pat Cummins cares about a lot of things. His family, his mates, the less fortunate, humanity, cricket. That may sound like and endorsement for sainthood. He wouldn't like that kind of accolade.

To sum it up simply, he cares.

COMETH THE MAN

India is a country I've come to love dearly over the years and the people here are some of the warmest and kindest I've ever met.

To know so many are suffering so much at this time saddens me greatly.

There has been quite a bit of discussion over here as to whether it is appropriate for the IPL to continue while COVID-19 infection rates remain high. I'm advised that the Indian Government is of the view that playing the IPL while the population is in lockdown provides a few hours of joy and respite each day at an otherwise difficult time for the country.

As players, we are privileged to have a platform that allows us to reach millions of people that we can use for good. With that in mind, I have made a contribution to the "PM Cares Fund," specifically to purchase oxygen supplies for India's hospitals.

I encourage my fellow IPL players - and anyone around else the world who has been touched by India's passion and generosity - to contribute. I will kick it off with $50,000.

At times like this it is easy to feel helpless. I've certainly felt that of late. But I hope by making this public appeal we can all channel our emotions into action that will bring light into people's lives.

I know my donation isn't much in the grand scheme of things, but I hope it will make a difference to someone.

The social media post by Pat Cummins about his donation.

17

PRINCIPLES AND CONSCIENCE

Sport and politics increasingly are intertwined. Not necessarily party politics – more it's a case of national and international issues spilling over into sport.

The banning of Russian athletes from world sports, or at least identifying as Russian in some major events, followed Russia's invasion of Ukraine in 2022.

That's the most obvious case. A widespread boycott of the Moscow Olympics in 1979 over the Russian invasion of Afghanistan (Russia seems to have form in this activity) was another case where political activism had a major effect on sport.

The Olympic Games in 1936 produced one of the earliest political statements by athletes.

The 10th modern Olympics held in Berlin from 1-16 August 1936 degenerated into a massive propaganda exercise by Adolf Hitler two years after he became Fuhrer.

Boycotts were threatened over Hitler's attitude to Jews. Despite assurances sought and given about not turning the games into a propaganda exercise, Germany still promoted Nazi ideology. Pamphlets and speeches about the superiority of the Aryan race were commonplace, and the Reich Sports Field that covered four stadiums was draped in German Reich (Nazi) banners and symbols.

The Olympics was a vehicle for protest in 1968. During the medal

PRINCIPLES AND CONSCIENCE

ceremony in Mexico City on 16 October 1968, two African-American athletes, Tommie Smith and John Carlos, each raised a black-gloved fist during the playing of the US national anthem. While on the podium, Smith and Carlos, who had won gold and bronze medals respectively in the 200-metres event turned to face the US flag and raised their fists. Smith, Carlos, and Australian silver medallist Peter Norman wore human-rights badges on their jackets.

In recent times, American footballer Colin Kaepernick caused controversy when he "took the knee" (going down on bended knee) during the national anthem before a match in 2016. He said he could not stand to show pride in the flag of a country that oppressed black people.

"Taking the knee" before sporting events became more common in the US in 2020 after the murder of George Floyd, an unarmed African American man who was killed during an arrest by a white police officer.

The movement, in support of equality and a protest against racism, quickly spread worldwide with "Black Lives Matter" protests. The last words of Floyd – "I can't breathe" also became a symbol in protests.

Taking a knee also appeared in Australia in sporting events.

Australia's cricket team joined the West Indies in taking the knee in Perth before the start of a Test match in Perth in November 2022.

The two teams earlier took part in a Barefoot Circle to acknowledge the traditional owners of the land.

Cummins rubbished concerns his team was becoming too outspoken on social issues.

"In this position you're always going upset people, whether you do something or you don't do something," Cummins said.

"That's fine. I kind of know what I signed up for. I also think we're cricket players, but you can't leave your values at the door.

"People stand for different things, and something like taking a knee this week we're doing it out of respect for the West Indies, in support of equality."

That's not the only social issue in which Cummins has become a prominent figure.

He joined around 300 Australian athletes in the "Cool Down initiative" to draw attention to climate change.

The Cool Down web page explains: "We are a sporting nation. We play sport, we watch sport, we love sport.

"From the Boxing Day Test to footy finals fever. From early mornings paddling out at breaks around the country to park runs in hundreds of cities and towns.

"But the climate crisis and Australia's intensifying extreme weather is threatening the sports and country we love.

"We've seen Australia's extreme weather become even more extreme. Outrageous temperatures at the Australian Open have forced early retirements and bushfire smoke has seen training and matches cancelled for safety. But it's our local clubs that are most feeling the heat.

"Dramatically rising insurance premiums to protect against expanding fire and flood risk are eating into budgets and prolonged droughts are seeing grounds become unusable and, in some cases, entire seasons being cancelled.

"Sport's future is more uncertain than ever, but its power has never been more important.

"Australians have always punched above our weight on the world stage and it's time to do it on climate. To safeguard the games we love for generations to come we must cut our emissions by at least half by 2030 and reach net-zero before 2050.

"Together, we can do this Australia – for the future of sport.

For the future of our great country. "

Cricket can use its platform to make a difference in combatting climate change despite its large carbon footprint, Cummins says.

In 2023 Cummins was named Athlete of the Year in the BBC Green Sport Awards.

"Cricket is a sport that is dependent on the weather," he told BBC Sport.

PRINCIPLES AND CONSCIENCE

"We sometimes play in conditions where it's 50 degrees and you physically cannot perform to anywhere near where you want to be, and we've had games that have been called off due to a bushfire in the middle of summer.

"The nature of international cricket means you travel around the world a lot, you have quite a high carbon footprint, so it's always front of mind."

Cummins told *The Australian* newspaper: "The game has a big footprint – we fly all over the world in jets, we've got big stadiums, play under massive lights, the fields use so much valuable water. There's a lot we can do. Sport will be affected, but cricket in particular, we are subject to the elements."

Cummins launched Cricket for Climate straight after the Ashes series in Australia, starting with his own club, Penrith.

The aim is to install solar power at 4,000 cricket clubs across Australia. He has hosted discussions among leaders of cricket and other sports about how cricket can reduce its carbon footprint.

"We've got to do our bit to make sure we try to limit temperature increases to as little as possible or else in the future cricket could be a lot harder to play," Cummins said.

He makes fair points about the effect of climate on cricket. What of the effect of cricket on climate?

Cricketers travelling the world, from one country to the next, be it for international matches or domestic leagues, contribute to the level of global warming and pollution that is attributed to aircraft.

A five-year research project led by the UK's Manchester Metropolitan University in collaboration with academic and research institutions across the world found that global air travel and transport was responsible for 3.5% of all drivers of climate change from human activities. Australian airline Qantas is the official airline of Cricket Australia.

The stance taken by Cummins on issues wasn't universally welcomed, some commentators taking an insular view that the Test captain should be focussed more on winning the Ashes.

Cummins and his principles gained more attention in 2023 when he said he would no longer appear in advertisements for Alinta Energy which was in the final year of a multi-million-dollar sponsorship agreement with Cricket Australia. He had appeared with other Australian cricketers in advertisements over the previous four years.

Alinta did not renew the agreement.

CA said the views of Cummins and others had no bearing on the split with Alinta. Ending the partnership came from Alinta due to a "change in its brand strategy", CA said.

For his part, Cummins rubbished suggestions his stance had cost Australian cricket a $40 million deal. "Complete rubbish," he said.

He also said he'd make no apologies for continuing his crusade for climate change.

He accepts he will be torn down on social media over his actions.

"It doesn't bother me at all," he said. "I am not doing things to please absolutely everyone."

When asked about taking a stance on issues, Cummins said: "It has always been a balance. We have seen certain players make decisions based on religions, or certain foods they eat, where they won't join specific partners.

"Every organisation has a responsibility to do what's right for the sport and what they think is right for the organisation and, I hope, society when it moves forward. It is a balance when you make decisions about who you are going to welcome into the cricket family."

Cummins has been outspoken on social issues in addition to climate change – the Yes vote in the Australia's Voice to Parliament referendum, and his team taking the knee the obvious ones.

Asked to expand on his community work, he says: "What motivates me is that I'm in a really lucky position so I try to help others if I can.

"I feel a responsibility to do some good because I'm in such a privileged position and not everyone is – I try not to lose sight of that."

His advocacy for social justice causes covers a wide spectrum, his

PRINCIPLES AND CONSCIENCE

profile as the nation's Test cricket captain an ideal platform to get his points across.

It isn't something that dominates his press conferences, but he is committed to making a difference.

"My generation and people around that are passionate about different things. They are open-minded to things…some people can't leave those values at the door. They can't walk past those values. If that creates difficult conversations maybe that is a good thing.

"I don't think I shout it from the roof tops. I just try and do a lot myself to make little changes in my life if I can. If I can make a little bit of difference through my actions or Cricket for Climate I am not too bothered by people picking holes in it.

"My job is to lead the team and do my best. If there are other things I am passionate about that I can think I can make a difference with then from time to time I can share them."

He supported women's cricketer Ash Gardner in her call for the date of Australia Day celebrations to be changed.

Indigenous star Gardner expressed her concerns about the date of the holiday as Australia prepared for a women's international match against Pakistan on Australia Day on 26 January 2023, in Hobart.

"I feel for Ash," Cummins said at the time. "It is a tough situation. It is a tough day for many in Australia."

Cricket Australia dropped the usual Australia Day Test from its promotion of the men's Test against the West Indies in Brisbane on 26 January 2024, drawing criticism as well as praise.

Cummins said speaking to fellow players including Gardner and Scott Boland had brought the issue closer to home.

"It (the issue) is not new," Cummins said. "This conversation comes up every year and Cricket Australia has been pretty consistent the last four or five years with the way they approach it.

"In a sport like cricket, which has such diversity and millions of people supporting it and playing it, you get a good spectrum of the community and a good feel for what the community expects.

"Knowing a couple of those players... you hear the stories and their feelings. So it does gather extra importance."

Cummins says he is not against having an Australia Day, but says a more suitable date would be appropriate.

Cricket Australia chief executive Nick Hockley said CA was trying to take a neutral position on the issue of 26 January.

"We are not precluding anybody celebrating Australia," Hockley said on radio. "We are not boycotting Australia Day.

"We are taking the same approach we have over the past four or five years. We have spoken to our players and spoken to our committee. We want people to come along and enjoy Australia Day.

"But for some, including in our elite playing group, it's not a day of celebration. And we are seeking to be as inclusive and welcoming as possible."

As well as environmental sustainability and Aboriginal issues, Cummins has advocated for mental health, calling for open conversations and encouraging people, particularly men, to talk about their mental well-being.

No one should doubt his sincerity, but there would be some commentators who would question the reliability of his source of information on indigenous issues. He has cited Bruce Pascoe's *Dark Emu* book as formative of his views about racism and indigenous issues.

Cummins' views may be legitimate but the source, Bruce Pascoe has come under question over his claimed authenticity, some saying he has failed to prove any Aboriginal heritage.

For his activism on causes that are close to his heart, including climate change, Cummins has been dubbed "Captain Planet" and "Captain Woke". To be fair that's far from a majority. It is more likely to be heard among those from bygone eras, those who regard themselves as "traditionalists" and who also didn't think a fast bowler could/should be captain of "their" Test side.

The negativity hasn't worried Cummins too much.

PRINCIPLES AND CONSCIENCE

"If I don't stay strong on this and I pander to a loud minority, that's not a good thing," he said.

Cummins conceded that the criticism sometimes took a toll. "I think you'd be lying if you said it doesn't," he said.

"I think you've got to find ways to manage it just like you manage your body as a professional athlete.

"You're not on an island. You can't just say, 'I want to play cricket in front of millions of people' but also 'I don't want anyone to have an opinion on me'. That's not what we sign up for.

"As long as I know I've got great relationships with teammates, family – they know who I am. I know who I am."

So where does the social conscience come from?

Cummins credits his family with helping him "keep his feet on the ground" after being appointed captain, the position once described by cricket tragic and then-Prime Minister John Howard as the second-most important position in Australia after the prime ministership.

"Mum and Dad were always trying to remind us how lucky we are to live in this country and have all the opportunities that we have, but also how we're just one small, little part of a very big world – and make sure we open our eyes," he said in an interview with the ABC.

"I think being part of big families helps. I've got two brothers, two sisters, and if you're starting to get too big for your boots they're willing to cut you down.

"We never took anything too seriously. Sport was always played because it was fun, and definitely competitive. I was trying to always keep up with my older brothers. I was always playing catch-up. There were no handicaps.

"Then as soon as it wasn't fun, you're doing it wrong. So I've always tried to hang on to that, even now. It's trying to find a bit of balance between cricket and normal life.

"And if cricket is becoming too stressful or too much, I've probably taken it a bit too seriously."

Achieving that balance has meant side-stepping some of the

lucrative deals on offer in some forms of the game, although he has done quite nicely out of his IPL contracts.

The money wouldn't loom large in his thoughts. His net worth has been put at from A$40-60 million by the financial press.

And when he has been available to play in the money-rich Indian Premier League, teams have been willing to pick him up at auction, at record prices.

He was at the top of his earning capacity in 2024, with a lucrative IPL contract in his pocket. What about the name-calling for some of his views?

Does any of that change his demeanour or distract from his aim of winning cricket matches?

No.

18

LOOKING AHEAD

In a perfect world, if my form and body could keep up I'd like to be playing into my mid-30s, I'd doubt that I'll be captaining that long. It's good to have some freshness every x amount of time. If I've got seven or eight years, in a perfect world, of Test cricket I'd be very surprised if I'm captain for the whole time.

PAT CUMMINS, *SYDNEY MORNING HERALD*, **FEBRUARY 2024**

Pat Cummins isn't thought likely to stand down from the captaincy any time soon. It isn't possible to predict his future, of course, but the longer he goes on the closer comes the appointment of a successor.

The name raised at the end of 2023 is Travis Head. He's the same age as Cummins, so his captaincy prospects will turn a lot on how long his captain can keep up his express pace while managing the players.

Cummins has come up short of advocacy for Head but says he's in the frame. Other candidates will emerge, no doubt, but Head had everyone talking in 2024 after his heroics in short form cricket (including the ODI World Cup) and the 2023-24 Test series.

"He's always been a leader in our group, so we thought it was a good time to formally recognise that," Cummins said as the side prepared for the Perth Test in 2023 having named Head as a co-vice-captain.

"While nothing's imminent, Steve (Smith, 35) is not going to play forever. I dare say I'm not going to captain them forever, so we feel like we've got some responsibility to future-proof the team and start trying to give opportunities to other leaders.

"It doesn't guarantee anything, but we've given him a good opportunity. So, when you look through candidates for future captains, of course he's going to be right up there. And I know in my last couple of years before I became captain, being in some of those conversations as a vice-captain really helped fast-track my readiness."

Cummins said teammates "love" the personality Head brings.

"You see it in the way he plays his cricket," Cummins said. "There's a certain amount of freedom to it; he takes the game on, he enjoys it. He's always got a smile on his face, he never takes anything too seriously.

"He's great at bringing the team together for team morale, for putting his arm around players that need it. Sometimes you can mistake that for someone who's not a deep thinker about the game, but I think tactically, he's excellent."

Cricket has been something of a rollercoaster ride for Head, a career of highs and lows.

He was marked down as a prospect for greatness at a young age, making his debut in first-class cricket for his home state, South Australia, in a match away against Victoria on 2 February 2012, having just turned 19. He scored 12 runs.

In February 2015, Head was named captain of South Australia; at 21 years old he was the youngest captain of the South Australian side in 122-years.

Head became something of an all-rounder, batting left-handed, bowling off-breaks and sometimes keeping wicket. He has played first-class cricket, including Tests as well as ODIs and T20s (including the IPL). He has opened in short-form games and generally bats in the middle order in Tests.

He remains contracted to South Australia for first-class cricket and to the Strikers in the Big Bash T20 competition.

He received his first Cricket Australia contract in 2017 and made

LOOKING AHEAD

his Test debut in 2018. He was quite disappointed in 2021 when his CA contract wasn't renewed.

He had been co-vice-captain with Pat Cummins to Tim Paine from January 2019 to November 2020.

He recalled: "I just look at probably a period of time which was around when I lost my contract. I went away for South Australia, played well and found myself back in the team around that Ashes series in (December) 2021."

It is fair to say that Cummins played a significant part in Head's progress through 2023 into 2024, something Head himself acknowledged.

"The change in guard with him being captain, and I guess the confidence he gave me to go out and play the way I do in domestic cricket. I probably look back (at that) as the moment when things turned," Head said of his resurrection. "And again, it's never guaranteed, but I was able to go out and get runs in that Test in Brisbane (he made 152)." He was also restored to a co-captaincy role, with Steve Smith, to Cummins.

The nub of his chat with Cummins was that he should forget that his place in the Test team was under scrutiny. Head went from "playing not to get out" to "playing to score runs," the result of the man-management skills of his skipper.

"I played probably a little bit more aggressively while I still worked hard on my technique and a few things. But I sort of hit a moment in the road where it didn't really matter if I didn't play for Australia again," he said. "I would love to have, but if it wasn't to be, it probably gave me a bit more of that more relaxed, comfortable sort of environment and attitude around things."

Head was in no doubt how that came about.

"In terms of leadership, around that Ashes series, he (Cummins) had a conversation with me around how he wanted to see me play and how he wanted me to go about it, which obviously we've seen the progress of and the results from – which has been nice. I think he's been really good," he says.

Joining the Sunrisers Hyderabad in the IPL in 2024 saw Head playing under Cummins again.

"I think a lot of guys obviously asked (me) about him leading into this IPL," Head said. "The Indian guys, when I got here, asked about what he's going to be like, and I said he would be really relaxed, be really calm and someone who talks a lot of sense. He's very measured and understands the game, and he's just really, really well-rounded off the field.

"He's really enjoyable to be around; he creates a really good environment. That's very inclusive. That's very enjoyable. That's very relaxed. And I think you're seeing that in the way we're playing that game style about being aggressive and relaxed. But I think you'll also be seeing guys play with a smile on their face and really stepping forward into that pressure. And I think that's what he's asking the guys to do."

Head was a hit in the 2024 IPL – in a game against Royal Challengers Bengaluru he slammed 102 runs from 41 balls (his century coming off 39). In 15 matches, he scored 567 runs at an average of 36.76. He scored one century and five fifties.

How long will it be before Cummins calls an end to his stellar career?

To look at him in 2024 in charge of any Australian team and even the Sunrisers Hyderabad in the IPL it is clear his is still enjoying life, as bowler and captain.

To be clear, nothing Pat Cummins has said indicated retirement was near. Travis Head may well keep his name in the frame, but the reality might be that by the time Cummins calls it a day, Head's chance may have passed.

There's an interesting point to be made about Australia's Test team. When Travis Head celebrated his 30th birthday on the last day of the Boxing Day Test in December 2023, only one player in the Australian side was in his 20s – Marnus Labuschagne, 29 years and 124 days old.

Cameron Green, 24, who didn't play in that Test, looks like becoming

LOOKING AHEAD

a regular Test player. He may well progress to a leadership role. There is a raft of younger players around Australia who would have Test cricket aspirations.

Usman Khawaja would turn 38 during the tour by India late in 2024, Nathan Lyon would turn 37, Steve Smith had turned 35 and Mitchell Starc also would be 35 by summer's end.

The oldest Australian men's team was that which played in the 1926 Ashes Test at Lord's with an average age just short of 36.

In Australia's 15-man squad for the T20 World Cup in the US and West Indies in 2024, 11 of them were 30 years old or older (average about 32). It would most likely be a quite different Australian team that lined up for the next T20 World Cup in 2026 in Sri Lanka and India.

Cummins was asked in early 2024 what changes might be on the cards for the 2024-25 Test matches and beyond.

"Realistically there is going to be some rate of change over the next couple of years," Cummins said. "We probably thought it was going to happen a little bit sooner, but everyone is hanging on."

Australia didn't have a heavy Test load through the middle of 2024.

"So I don't see anything in the immediate future that is going to change," Cummins said.

The team is well-established. Only 22 players have been used in the Test team in the 32 Tests while Cummins has been captain.

There has been no suggestion of any mass retirements yet, and Cummins was confident Australia could manage any changes in the squad over the next few years. He hoped the majority of his Test players would remain together while he was captain.

But when the time comes, where will the new crop of Tests players come from?

Cameron Green is top of the list, already a Test player and looking to become a permanent fixture. Todd Murphy (24) would also be in line for a spinning spot. Adam Zampa was the go-to bowler for leg-spin in the short-form games – would he also be a Test prospect or would Tanveer Sangha come into calculations for that role?

Wisden staff turned their minds to what Australia's team might look like in 2027-28.

One of the names they came up with was South Australian batter Nathan McSweeney (25), already tipped for higher honours by chair of selectors George Bailey. They thought 23-year-old NSW player Jack Edwards could be a contender in the all-rounder spot. Aaron Hardie was also thought to be a good prospect.

West Australian Teague Wyllie and South Australian Henry Hunt have been mentioned as potential openers.

The Big Bash has also brought attention to some players who might become Test stars, Jake Fraser-McGurk ahead on that list. Ollie Davis is another with potential.

The big questions related to fast bowlers.

"The Wild Thing" West Australian Lance Morris (26), rated as the fastest bowler going around in Australia in 2024, South Australian left-armer Spencer Johnson (28) and Queenslander Xavier Bartlett (25) have emerged as potential candidates for new-ball bowling.

All these names may well be in the mix. A problem for selectors is that they see more of them in the short-form game than the longer version. Elevation to the Test squad for any of those who light the flame in T20 or one-day cricket could make or break careers if they don't succeed.

Whoever does make the grade will no doubt be looking to skipper Pat Cummins for inspiration.

Australia was next to play a Test series at home, against India, in 2024-2025 (November to January), the first men's five-Test Match Border-Gavaskar Trophy Series since 1991-92.

ODIs and T20s were scheduled for Australia in England during September-October 2024 and in Pakistan in November.

Meanwhile, Cummins will stay calm and carry on.

In India, he spoke about staying calm. Was he born with the gift of calmness that has been a standout quality of his leadership in all forms?

"I think to some degree I was born with it. I have always kind of had this 'she'll be right' kind of attitude. The more I have played, the more I have mellowed a little bit in terms of not being as fiery, and you just want to concentrate on how to get the job done.

"As a young bowler I wanted to puff the chest out and really get into the opposition. Nowadays I'm a bit more about concentrating on my own game, and as captain trying to navigate as calmly as possibly our team to, hopefully, a victory. Maybe it is experience, maybe it is I try and talk about calmness a lot, so if I'm captain and I'm not calm, well, I'll lose a bit of credibility with my team-mates."

Is that a strength of a good leader? "I think so. On balance, when you are making so many decisions all the time, a level of calmness and consistency probably outweighs someone who's erratic, I would say."

Did signing up in June 2024 to the MLC franchise San Francisco unicorns give a hint to Cummins' plans?

His four-year deal would take him to 2027, possibly clashing with the June to August Ashes tour in England. He would then be 35.

MLC was being played through July in 2024, mainly because it followed the T20I World Cup.

If the season continues in July each year, Cummins could have to make an important call.

19

THERE'S SOMETHING ABOUT PAT

WHAT IS IT ABOUT CRICKET THAT DRIVES PAT CUMMINS?

There is nothing like it, the thrill of bowling fast, the crowd going crazy right behind you. You get a sense of teammates sensing something is happening – I love that. They say you don't have egos but we are super competitive and we all have egos.

We all want to be on the back pages of the paper, raising the bat or holding the ball up for five-for, being the match-winner. People will pretend that's not the case but you don't get to professional sport without a bit of that in you.

It's the adrenalin, trying to make a difference. Even thinking about it I start smiling.

PAT CUMMINS, FOX SPORT DOCUMENTARY, *THE MAKING OF PAT CUMMINS*.

The Fox Cricket documentary explained Pat Cummins' approach to cricket nicely.

It's the thrill of the chase.

He is a fierce competitor. It is hard to name a fast bowler who isn't.

A bowler smiling towards a batter as he runs in to fire down a projectile at 140 km/h at him isn't being nice. He's looking forward to seeing the batter squirm – duck, prod…and get out.

THERE'S SOMETHING ABOUT PAT

Away from the pitch the Cummins smile is not about striking terror into the mind of the recipient. It reflects his real persona.

Just a couple of examples of his care for his players: making sure Usman Khawaja wasn't excluded from Ashes Test celebrations, and running water to the players during the first T20 World Cup match against Oman when he wasn't named in the team.

Of course, cricket is much more than bowlers, batters and fielders out on a green field on a (hopefully) pleasant day.

On and off the field, there are magic moments, tragic moments and history-making moments.

To many people cricketers can be heroes. To others they might be villains (in a nice way of course).

But they are real people.

The Test—a documentary series that followed the Australian team's tour of UK in 2023, provided an insight into the goings-on behind the scenes.

Why do it?

"One of the reasons why we sign up for doing these series is that it does show different sides of the players," Cummins said afterwards.

"When I was a kid, all I wanted to know was, what the cricketers do off the field and in the change room, all those kind of little anecdotal things about the players.

"So I hope…people who watch this series feel like they're closer to the players, they get a bit more of context of what makes the players tick. Maybe they're a little bit more understanding if things don't go right."

Cummins has experienced ups and down – not just on the cricket pitch – incidents and events that have affected him deeply, some others that he will remember forever.

The most notable, of course, was the passing of his mother Maria in 2023. Cummins rushed home from India to be with his family. That's where he belonged, and he was right to go home.

For Pat Cummins the loss of his mother hit hard.

PAT CUMMINS

The cricket world rallied around Cummins once the seriousness of his mother's illness became known.

The Barmy Army posted a video of their trumpeter playing "Maria" from West Side Story during the second Test between England and New Zealand.

"This is amazing, thank you," Cummins replied. "Mum loved watching this and felt very touched."

Fast bowler Mitchell Starc had gone through something similar. He said the cricket community had been incredibly supportive after the loss of his father Paul, who died of cancer a matter of weeks after the 2020-21 series against India.

"Having been through a similar situation recently, it's a hard place to be," Starc said of his Test teammate and skipper. "Trying to get your head around playing international cricket and for him to captain at the same time when your mind might be back home or with your family.

"We're sons, partners, fathers first, people first, and cricketers second. He's got the complete support of the group. It's been tough to see him go through it from afar, so nice for him to get the opportunity to go home, be around the family, support the rest of his family and to go through that."

After Maria passed, players wore black armbands. Condolences came from near and far. The Australian team had been in India and one of those to offer tributes was former Indian captain Sunil Gavaskar

"May I please offer my condolences to Pat Cummins on the loss of his mother," Gavaskar said on Fox Cricket.

"It is something that I have undergone recently. I lost my mother on Christmas Day and…in the immediate aftermath you don't seem to realise (the magnitude of the loss) because you're so caught up with the last rites…(but as the days go by), you start missing a little bit more.

"Condolences to Pat and may her soul rest in eternal peace."

All the messages were a tribute to the esteem in which Pat Cummins is held the world of cricket where the game is competitive and sometimes controversial.

THERE'S SOMETHING ABOUT PAT

Cummins was willing to talk about the loss of his mother: "So many people have similar stories, and I think I know them telling me about how they've kind of dealt with it and gone through it certainly helped me kind of rationalise it.

"So if I can help some other people down the track by speaking about it, potentially I will."

Cummins spoke about the death of his mother in an interview on social media platform Weare8 with former England professional footballer Rio Ferdinand.

He told of his son Albie and the last meeting the two had with Maria in March 2023.

Cummins was asked to take a sentimental item to the interview. He chose a children's book his mother had read to his son in their final moments together.

"I'm not a very sentimental person so I had to think what in the house was important to me," Cummins said.

"I brought a kids' book. My son Albie is 18 months old. It's his favourite kids' book. It's called *Birds*... he absolutely loves this book.

"Just before Mum passed away, this is the book Mum read to him the last time he saw her, so it's really special for me. My wife (Beckie) bought it so there's a huge connection that brings us all together."

He has also paid tribute to players that Australia lost – Phillip Hughes, Andrew Symonds, Rod Marsh and Shane Warne included. Those losses would have affected him deeply and were losses that had a big impact on the Australian cricket community, reflected in the tributes of Cummins.

There were moments of great joy away from the cricket pitch. His marriage to Rebecca and the birth of son Albie among the best.

He spoke often of the legacy he and the team were creating – the World Test Championship and the World ODI Cup victories would be long remembered.

His career shouldn't be over any time soon but when it is he will have some fantastic cricket memories. So will cricket fans.

He will have made a difference.

EPILOGUE
The Cummins philosophy on cricket:

"You have to make sure you find a way to keep enjoying it. As a kid, I'd play every day in the backyard because I loved it. It wasn't because I thought I've got to do this for a career. It's always about the love of the game."

The Cummins philosophy on life:

"To soar, you must do two things: have the courage to spread your wings, and release the weights holding you down."

And: "I can accept failure. Everyone fails at something. But I can't accept not trying."

20

THE CUMMINS FILE

Patrick James Cummins

BORN: 09 May 1993, Westmead, Sydney. Raised: Mount Riverview, Blue Mountains, west of Sydney.

PARENTS: Peter and Maria (Maria passed away 10/03/23)

My mother told me… *"Pat, go and take on the world. Someone's going to go and do these wonderful things, it might as well be you."*

– Pat Cummins, Season 3 of the documentary *The Test*

SIBLINGS: Matt, Tim, Laura, Kara.

SCHOOLS: St Paul's Grammar.

CRICKET CLUBS: Glenbrook Blaxland CC (junior) then Penrith (first grade 2010).

CHILDHOOD CRICKET IDOL: Brett Lee (went on to play with him in domestic and international matches).

THE YOUNG LEGEND: An opposition player's mother asked the 13-year-old Cummins to stop bowling so fast because he kept hitting her son. When he was 14, a bail from the stumps supposedly flew over the fence after he clean-bowled someone.

UNIVERSITY: University of Technology, Sydney, Elite Athlete Program. Graduated 2017 with a Bachelor of Business degree.

SPOUSE: Becky (Boston).

NICKNAMES: Cider, Cummo.

CHILDREN: Albie (son, 2021).

PAT CUMMINS

SOCIAL MEDIA: 2.5mil followers Facebook. Profile: "Dad to Albie, Australian Cricket Captain, Pretend Farmer, Whisky Lover."

HEIGHT: 192 cm.

BOWLING: Right arm fast (very).

BEST YEAR AS A TEST BOWLER: 2019, 59 wickets at 20.14.

BATTING: Right-hand

BEST YEAR AS A TEST BATTER: 2023, 254 runs at 15.88.

OFFICIAL FASTEST RECORDED DELIVERY: v England, 2017, 149.2 km/h.

TEAMS: Tests: Australia.

Indian Premier League: Sunrisers Hyderabad, Delhi Daredevils, Kolkata Knight Riders, Mumbai Indians.

State: New South Wales Second XI, New South Wales.

Big Bash (Australia): Perth Scorchers, Sydney Sixers, Sydney Thunder.

AUSTRALIAN DEBUTS: ODI, South Africa vs Australia at Centurion – October 19, 2011 (cap 189); T20I, South Africa vs Australia at Cape Town – October 13, 2011 (cap 51); Test, South Africa vs Australia at Johannesburg – November 17-21, 2011 (cap 423).

FIRST CLASS DEBUT: NSW vs Tasmania at Hobart – March 03-05, 2011. List A debut: NSW vs Queensland at North Sydney – February 13, 2011.

DOMESTIC T20 DEBUT: Tasmania vs NSW at Sydney – January 19, 2011

TEST RECORD (to June 2024): 62 Tests for 269 wickets at an average of 22.54 (approx. 2.88 per over). Best bowling innings – 6 for 23 (against Sri Lanka in Brisbane in 2019). Number 1 ranked bowler 2019-2023.

ODI RECORD: 88 matches for 141 wickets at an average of 28.67 (approx. 5.29 per over). Best bowling innings – 5 for 70 (against India in Chandigarh, 2019).

T20 INTERNATIONALS: 52 matches for 57 wickets at an average of 24.77 (almost 7.43 runs per over). Best bowling innings – 3 for 15 (against Pakistan in Dubai, 2012).

THE CUMMINS FILE

ICC BOWLING RANKINGS: JUNE 2024: Test – 5th. ODIs – 29th. T20s – 47th.

AUSTRALIAN CAPTAINCY RECORD (21 November 2021 to June 2024):

Tests – 32 matches, 20 wins, 6 losses, 6 drawn.

ODIs – 15 matches, 12 wins, 3 losses.

IPL RECORD (2014-24): 58 matches, 515 runs, av 22.67, HS 35 no; 219 overs, 566 runs, 63 wickets, av 31.44.

SHIRT NUMBERS: 30 (Australia and IPL).

ENDORSEMENTS: Gilette, Carrera. New Balance, Kayo, UNICEF, Lyre's Spirit, Nexba, WeAre8, Rario, Dr Electrify.

CRICKET AUSTRALIA CONTRACT: $3 million (est.) 2024.

AWARDS:

ICC Men's Test Cricketer of the Year: 2019; Sir Garfield Sobers Trophy (men's cricketer of the year): 2023.

Allan Border Medal: 2019.

ICC Men's Test Team of the Year: 2019, 2022, 2023 (captain).

Shane Warne Men's Test Player of the Year: 2021.

Wisden Leading Cricketer of the World: 2023.

CAREER BOWLING STATISTICS

FORMAT		Mat	Inns	Overs	Mdns	Runs	Wkts	BBM	Avg	Econ	SR	5w	10w
Tests	2011-2024	62	115	2102.2	464	6063	269	10/62	22.53	2.88	46.8	12	2
ODIs	2011-2023	88	88	763.5	44	4042	141	5/70	28.66	5.29	32.5	1	0
T20Is	2011-2024	52	52	190.0	3	1412	57	3/15	24.77	7.43	20.0		

To June 2024

TIMELINE

3 Jan 2010: Represents NSW at the National Under-17 Championships. Later plays Under-19 cricket for NSW aged 17. Makes his Futures League debut for NSW in late 2010.

20 Jan 2011: Makes senior State debut after five Second XI matches for NSW. Takes three wickets for NSW in a Big Bash match against Tasmania in Sydney. Speed gun records 140 km/h plus delivery. Plays six games in the 2011 Big Bash, including the final, and is the equal-leading wicket-taker with 11.

13 Feb 2011: Makes List A debut for NSW against Queensland at North Sydney Oval. Six overs cost 25 runs, 0 wickets.

3 Mar 2011: First-class debut in Sheffield Shield game against Tasmania. Plays in NSW's last three matches of the season, including the final in Hobart, bowling 65 overs.

23 May 2011: Ruled out of Australia A's tour of Zimbabwe with a back injury.

7 Jun 2011: Awarded one of 25 Cricket Australia contracts, a month after his 18th birthday.

28 Sep 2011: While playing for NSW in the T20 Champions League in South Africa is called into Australia's ODI and T20 squads for matches against the home team.

13 Oct 2011: International debut in Cape Town in the first T20I, taking 3-25 from four overs. Plays five of the six white-ball games on the tour, leading all bowlers with 10 wickets.

17 Oct 2011: Named in Australia's squad for the two-Test series against South Africa (after three first-class matches).

17 Nov 2011: Doesn't play in Australia's record-breaking loss in the first Test in Cape Town but replaces injured Ryan Harris for the second Test. Receives "Baggy Green" from former captain Ricky Ponting. Aged just 18 years and 193 days, Cummins is the second-youngest man to play Test cricket for Australia behind Ian Craig (1953).

THE CUMMINS FILE

21 Nov 2011: In the Wanderers Test, Cummins walks to the wicket with Australia eight wickets down and needing 18 runs to win. He clubs two boundaries and is 13 not out as Australia win. In the first innings he claimed his first Test wicket, Hashim Amla and follows up in the second innings with 6-79 to turn the match in Australia's favour. Wins player of the match award.

24 Nov 2011: Reveals he played through the pain of a serious heel injury during his debut series. Misses the 2011-12 home summer season. Returned to Australian representation in Australia's Under 19 side in April 2012.

28 Oct 2012: He is in the Sydney Sixers side that wins that year's T20 Champions League title in South Africa. Returning to Australia, scans reveal a stress fracture in his back. He misses the home season for the second successive year.

19 Aug 2013: Plays some matches for Australia A but is again ruled out of the international home season with a flare-up of the stress injury in his back. He plays only three games of cricket between October 2012 and his return to the Big Bash in January 2014. Works with fast-bowling legend Dennis Lillee to correct his action so he can avoid further injuries.

October 2013: On a quiet Sunday night out in Sydney, he meets Rebecca Boston, a 22-year-old from Harrogate in England, who is on a working holiday in Australia.

20 May 2014: He plays his first match in the Indian Premier League for Kolkata Knight Riders who went on to win the league. More than 80,000 fans turn up to KKR's home stadium the next day to celebrate with the team.

29 Mar 2015: Is relatively injury-free in 2014 and concentrates on short-form cricket. Named in Australia's squad that goes on to win the ODI World Cup at the MCG. Plays four games, replaced by Josh Hazlewood for the knockout stage.

PAT CUMMINS

13 July 2015: Ryan Harris is a late withdrawal from Australia's Ashes squad and Cummins is called in even though he hasn't played first-class cricket in almost two years. Fails to gain selection in an Ashes match.

24 Sep 2015: He suffers another serious back injury in the ODIs in England after the Test series and for the fourth time in five years is ruled out of the home season.

7 Oct 2016: He returns to the NSW side for the One-Day Cup and the team wins the title. He plays 25 short-form matches for Australia and the Big Bash in four-and-a-half months as he builds towards a return to first-class cricket.

26 Feb 2017: He is back from a three-match T20I series in Sri Lanka and stars for his club side, Penrith, in a thrilling one-run victory over Hawkesbury in the McDonald's First Grade Limited-Overs Cup Final. Cummins bowled the last over with Penrith needing one wicket and Hawkesbury needing five runs. A run-out gives Penrith victory.

7 Mar 2017: He returns to the Sheffield Shield competition for the first time in six years. He takes eight wickets in 36 overs against South Australia at the SCG.

11 Mar 2017: He returns to the Test squad for the tour of India. Replaces the injured Mitchell Starc in the final two Tests of the series. He bowls 79 overs in two weeks and joins the Indian Premier League series afterwards. Misses only two of Australia's next 33 Tests.

8 Jan 2018: He plays in Australia's 4-0 Ashes victory over England at home. Plays in all five Tests and tops the bowling with 23 wickets from around 200 overs in the series.

01 Apr 2018: Scores his first Test half-century in first innings v South Africa at Johannesburg. Takes 9-141 for the match which South Africa won by 492 runs.

9 Aug 2018: Having missed the 2018 IPL season with yet another back injury, he is also ruled out of the away Test tour against Pakistan.

THE CUMMINS FILE

28 Sep 2018: Australia's top players take part in a ballot to identify leaders within the extended group. The top six were Tim Paine, Aaron Finch, Travis Head, Alex Carey, Josh Hazlewood and Mitch Marsh. Cummins is overlooked. Hazlewood and Marsh are named co vice-captains of the Test team.

01 Jan 2019: He says the notion of him becoming national captain is "ridiculous."

22 Jan 2019: He and Travis Head are named vice-captains for the Tests against Sri Lanka. Tim Paine is captain.

11 Feb 2019: He wins the Allan Border Medal as Australia's most outstanding male cricketer.

17 Feb 2019: He is No.1 in the ICC's Test bowling rankings, the first Australian to reach the top since Glenn McGrath in 2006. He plays in all six Tests in the 2018-19 summer. He takes 6-29 in the second-innings of the first Test against Sri Lanka in Brisbane.

6 Aug 2019: He takes his 100th career wicket – Johnny Bairstow, at Edgbaston at the start of the 2019 Ashes. Cummins plays all five Tests as Australia retain the Ashes Urn on UK soil for the first time since 2001.

19 Dec 2019: He is bought for A$3.1m by KKR in the Indian Premier League auction, at the time the most expensive purchase for an overseas player in the tournament's history.

31 Dec 2019: He completes the calendar year with 99 wickets – 59 in Tests, 31 in ODIs and nine in T20 Internationals.

15 Jan 2020: He is named Test Player of the Year (2019) by the International Cricket Council (ICC).

29 Feb 2020: He takes his 100th ODI wicket, against South Africa in South Africa.

18 Aug 2020: He is named Australia's vice-captain for the white-ball tour of England. In November, Head is no longer vice-captain of the Test team, replaced by Cummins as Paine's deputy.

15 Feb 2021: He makes his captaincy debut for NSW in a Marsh One-

PAT CUMMINS

Day Cup game in Sydney. The NSW Blues win.

15 Nov 2021: He is in the Australian team that wins the men's T20 World Cup for the first time, taking five wickets at an economy rate of 7.37.

26 Nov 2021: He is named Australia's 47th Test captain, after the resignation of Tim Paine a week earlier. He is the first Australian fast bowler to be appointed permanent captain in 144 years of Test cricket. Leads Australia to 4-0 home series Ashes win over England.

6 Apr 2022: Playing for KKR in the IPL he smashes a 14-ball half-century, equalling the record for fastest fifty in the history of the tournament.

8 Oct 2022: Pat and Becky's son Albie is born.

11 Jun 2023: He leads Australia to victory in the World Test Championship final against India.

29 July 2022: Pat Cummins marries Becky Boston in Byron Bay.

19 Nov 2023: He leads Australia to an upset six-wickets win in the final of the ODI World Cup against India in India, after opting to bowl first. Cummins took 2-34 in his 10 overs without conceding a boundary. He contributed just 12 runs from 68 balls in a 202-runs partnership with Glenn Maxwell to seal a win over Afghanistan in the preliminary rounds and go into the semi-finals. Maxwell went on to make an unbeaten 201.

29 Dec 2023: Australia defeats Pakistan at home to claim the Test series 2-0. Cummins took 10 wickets for the match in the second Test, also claiming his 250th Test wicket.

4 Mar 2024: Sunrisers Hyderabad name Pat Cummins as captain of the team for the Indian Premier League season. SRH bought Cummins at the IPL auction for A$3.67m.

15 April 2024: Wisden names Pat Cummins as Leading Cricketer in the World for 2023.

18 May 2024: After finishing last of 10 in 2023, Sunrisers Hyderabad, led by Cummins and coached by Australian assistant coach and former NZ Test player Daniel Vettori, reach the 2024 final-four play-offs in the

THE CUMMINS FILE

IPL. SRH lose Qualifier 1 but win Qualifier 2 to face KKR again in the final.

26 May 2024: KKR with Mitch Starc in top form defeat the Cummins-led SRH in the IPL final. Starc took 2-24 and Cummins topped score in the losing side with 24.

28 May 2024: Pat Cummins, Mitchell Starc, Travis Head miss Australia's warm-up matches of the T20 World Cup 2024. The World Cup starts on 1 June. Mitch Marsh is captain of the Australians, and defeat Oman in their first match. Cummins did not play in the first game.

21 and 23 June 2024: Cummins takes a hat-trick in back-to-back games at the T20 World Cup, against Bangladesh and Afghanistan. Afghanistan went on to reach the semi-finals at the expense of Australia.

ENDORSEMENTS, PROMOTIONS AND BRANDS

Pat Cummins has been involved in a range of associations and campaigns. These are some, past and present:

New Balance, sports gear; Gillette, shaving; UNICEF Australia, ambassador; Carrer, eyewear brand ambassador; Kayo Sports, sports streaming network; Lyre's Spirit, non-alcoholic beverage; Nexba (sugar-free soft-drinks) and Goodness Group shareholder and brand ambassador; WeAre8, social media platform; Rario, marketplace for digital cricket collectables; Dr Electrify, Dr Saul Griffith's electrification blueprint for "The Big Switch"; Mawde, clothing brand; Gatorade, energy drink; Fox Cricket, Australian broadcaster; David Jones, promotion; Exclusive Style, clothing brand; Smile Foundation, South African children's health program; Optus Sport, infomercial promotion; Healthquad, health and fitness; Hublot, Swiss watchmaker.

Sources of information for this book include: Cricket Australia; ESPNcricinfo; howstat; cricket.com.au; crickbuzz.com; icc-cricket.com; interviews conducted by Ron Reed; Wisden; match broadcasts; media news and sport reports including the BBC and ABC; press conferences (ASAP Transcripts) and sources identified in text.

21

THE CUMMINS COLLECTION

Pat Cummins took over as permanent Test captain on 26 November 2021, the 47th leader of the team. He was appointed captain of the ODI team on 18 October 2022.

Between assuming the captaincy and the start of the T20 World Cup in 2024 (where he wasn't captain), he played across all forms of the international game.

His first task was the Ashes series against the visiting English team in December 2021.

Through 2022, he played in the final matches of the Ashes series and Test series against Pakistan, Sri Lanka, West Indies and South Africa.

The next year, 2023, was a stellar year for Cummins and the Australians.

He also played ODIs and T20 matches, though not many of the latter.

This was Australia's record in all forms from the Cummins Test captaincy appointment onwards to June 2024:

THE CUMMINS COLLECTION

2021

8 December: First Ashes Test v England (in Australia). Australia won by 9 wickets.

16 December: Second Ashes Test v England, Australia won by 275 runs.

26 December: Third Ashes Test v England. Australia won by an innings and 14 runs.

2022

5 January: Fourth Ashes Test v England. Drawn.

14 January: Fifth Ashes Test v England, Australia won by 146 runs.

11 February: First T20I v Sri Lanka. Australia won by 20 runs (D/L method).

13 February: Second T20I v Sri Lanka. Australia won in super over.

15 February: Third T20I v Sri Lanka. Australia won by 20 runs.

18 February: Fourth T20I v Sri Lanka. Australia won by 6 wickets.

20 February: Fifth T20I v Sri Lanka. Sri Lanka won by 5 wickets.

4 March: First Test in Pakistan. Pakistan v Australia. Drawn.

12 March: Second Test Pakistan v Australia. Drawn.

21 March: Third Test Pakistan v Australia. Australia won by 115 runs.

29 March: First ODI Pakistan v Australia. Australia won by 88 runs.

31 March: Second ODI Pakistan v Australia. Pakistan won by 6 wickets.

2 April: Third ODI Pakistan v Australia. Pakistan won by 9 wickets.

*Pat Cummins did not play in series. Andrew McDonald began as interim coach.

6 April: One-off T20I. Pakistan v Australia. Australia won by 3 wickets.

*Pat Cummins did not play in this match.

7 June: First T20I Sri Lanka v Australia. Australia won by 10 wickets.

*Andrew McDonald's first series as permanent coach.

8 June: Second T20I Sri Lanka v Australia. Australia won by 3 wickets.

11 June: Third T20I Australia v Sri Lanka. Sri Lanka won by 4 wickets.

*Pat Cummins did not play in this series.

14 June: First ODI Sri Lanka v Australia. Australia won by 2 wickets (D/L).

PAT CUMMINS

16 June: Second ODI Sri Lanka v Australia. Sri Lanka won by 26 runs (D/L).

19 June: Third ODI Sri Lanka v Australia. Sri Lanka won by 6 wickets.

21 June: Fourth ODI Sri Lanka v Australia. Sri Lanka won by 4 runs.

24 June: Fifth ODI Sri Lanka v Australia. Australia won by 4 wickets.

29 June: First Test Sri Lanka v Australia. Australia won by 10 wickets.

8 July: Second Test Sri Lanka v Australia. Sri Lanka won by 39 runs.

28 August: First ODI Australia v Zimbabwe. Australia won by 5 wickets.

31 August: Second ODI Australia v Zimbabwe. Australia won by 8 wickets.

3 September: Third ODI Australia v Zimbabwe. Zimbabwe won by 3 wickets.

* Pat Cummins did not play in this series.

6 September: First ODI Australia v New Zealand. Australia won by 2 wickets.

8 September: Second ODI Australia v New Zealand. Australia won by 113 runs.

11 September: Third ODI Australia v New Zealand. Australia won by 25 runs.

*Pat Cummins did not play in this series.

20 September: First T20I India v Australia. Australia won by 4 wickets.

23 September: Second T20I India v Australia. India won by 6 wickets.

25 September: Third T20I India v Australia. India won by 6 wickets.

*Aaron Finch was captain. Pat Cummins played.

5 October: First T20I Australia v West Indies. Australia won by 3 wickets.

7 October: Second T20I Australia v West Indies. Australia won by 31 runs.

*Finch was captain. Pat Cummins played.

9 October: First T20I Australia v England. England won by 8 runs.

12 October: Second T20I Australia v England. England won by 8 runs.

14 October: Third T20I Australia v England. Match abandoned.

*Finch was captain. Pat Cummins played in matches 2 and 3.

THE CUMMINS COLLECTION

17 October: T20 World Cup warm-up: Australia v India. India won by 6 wickets.

*Pat Cummins did not play.

22 October: World Cup T20 Australia v New Zealand. New Zealand won by 89 runs.

25 October: World Cup T20 Australia v Sri Lanka. Australia won by 7 wickets.

28 October: World Cup T20 Australia v England. Match abandoned.

31 October: World Cup T20 Australia v Ireland. Australia won by 42 runs.

4 November: World Cup T20 Australia v Afghanistan. Australia won by 4 runs.

*Finch was captain. Pat Cummins played. Australia eliminated on net run rate.

17 November: First ODI Australia v England. Australia won by 6 wickets.

*Pat Cummins' first match as ODI captain.

19 November: Second ODI Australia v England. Australia won by 92 runs.

22 November: Third ODI Australia v England. Australia won by 221 runs (D/L).

30 November: First Test Australia v West Indies. Australia won by 164 runs.

8 December: Second Test Australia v West Indies. Australia won by 419 runs.

17 December: First Test Australia v S. Africa. Australia won by 6 wickets.

26 December: Second Test Australia v S. Africa. Australia won by an innings and 182 runs.

2023

4 January: Third Test Australia v S. Africa. Drawn.

9 February: First Test India v Australia. India won by 132 runs.

17 February: Second Test India v Australia. India won by 6 wickets.

1 March: Third Test India v Australia. Australia won by 9 wickets.

9 March: Fourth Test India v Australia. Drawn.

PAT CUMMINS

17 March: First ODI India v Australia. India won by 5 wickets.

19 March: Second ODI India v Australia. Australia won by 10 wickets.

22 March: Third ODI India v Australia. Australia won by 21 runs.

7 June: World Test Championship Final: India v Australia. Australia won by 209 runs.

16 June: First Ashes Test England v Australia. Australia won by 2 wickets.

28 June: Second Ashes Test England v Australia. Australia won by 2 wickets.

6 July: Third Ashes Test England v Australia. England won by 3 wickets.

19 July: Fourth Ashes Test England v Australia. Drawn.

27 July: Fifth Ashes Test England v Australia. England won by 49 runs.

21 August: First T20I S. Africa v Australia. Australia won by 11 runs.

2 September: Second T20I S. Africa v Australia. Australia won by 8 wickets.

3 September: Third T20I S. Africa v Australia. Australia won by 5 wickets.

*Pat Cummins did not play.

7 September: First ODI S. Africa v Australia. Australia won by 3 wickets.

9 September: Second ODI S. Africa v Australia. Australia won by 123 runs.

12 September: Third ODI S. Africa v Australia. S. Africa won by 111 runs.

15 September: Fourth ODI S. Africa v Australia. S. Africa won by 164 runs.

17 September: Fifth ODI S. Africa v Australia. S. Africa won by 122 runs.

*Pat Cummins did not play.

22 September: First ODI India v Australia. India won by 5 wickets.

24 September: Second ODI India v Australia. India won by 99 runs (D/L).

*Pat Cummins did not play in Second ODI.

27 September: Third ODI India v Australia. Australia won by 66 runs.

3 October: ODI World Cup warm-up Australia v Pakistan. Australia won by 14 runs.

THE CUMMINS COLLECTION

ODI WORLD CUP 2023, INDIA

8 October: India defeated Australia by 6 wickets
12 October: South Africa d Australia by 134 runs.
20 October: Australia d Pakistan by 62 runs.
25 October: Australia d Netherlands by 309 runs.
27 October: Australia d New Zealand by 5 runs
4 November: Australia d England by 33 runs.
7 November: Australia d Afghanistan by 8 wickets.
11 November: Australia d Bangladesh by 8 wickets
16 November (2nd semi): Australia d South Africa by 3 wickets.
19 November (final): Australia d India by 6 runs.

14 December: First Test Australia v Pakistan. Australia won by 360 runs.
26 December: Second Test Australia v Pakistan. Australia won by 79 runs.

2024

3 January: Third Test Australia v Pakistan. Pakistan won by 8 wickets.
17 January: First Test Australia v W. Indies. Australia won by 10 wickets.
25 January: Second Test Australia v W. Indies. W. Indies won by 8 runs (D/L).
2 February: First ODI Australia v W. Indies. Australia won by 8 wickets.
4 February: Second ODI Australia v W. Indies. Australia won by 83 runs.
6 February: Third ODI Australia v W. Indies. Australia won by 8 wickets.
*Pat Cummins did not play.
9 February: First T20I Australia v W. Indies. Australia won by 11 runs.
11 February: Second T20I Australia v W. Indies. Australia won by 34 runs.
13 February: Third T20I Australia v W. Indies. W. Indies won by 37 runs.
*Pat Cummins did not play.
21 February: First T20I NZ v Australia. Australia won by 6 wickets.
23 February: Second T20I NZ v Australia. Australia won by 72 runs.

PAT CUMMINS

25 February: Third T20I NZ v Australia. Australia won by 27 runs (D/L).
*Mitch Marsh was captain, Pat Cummins played.
29 February: First Test NZ v Australia. Australia won by 172 runs.
8 March: Second Test NZ v Australia. Australia won by 3 wickets.

T20 WORLD CUP 2024

6 June: Australia v Oman. Australia won by 39 runs.
*Pat Cummins did not play.
9 June: Australia v England. Australia won by 36 runs. (Cummins 2-23).
11 June: Australia v Namibia. Australia won by 9 wickets (Namibia all out 72 in 10 overs. Zampa 4-12; Cummins 1-16).
15 June: Australia v Scotland. Australia won by 5 wickets.
*Pat Cummins did not play.
21 June, Super 8s: Australia v Bangladesh. Australia won by 28 runs DLS. (Cummins 3-29; hat-trick).
23 June, Super 8s: Australia v Afghanistan. Afghanistan won by 21 runs (Cummins 3-38 – 4 overs; completing back-to-back hat-tricks).
25 June, Super 8s: Australia v India. India won by 24 runs (Cummins 0-48) – 4 overs).

Cummins played five T20 World Cup matches, taking nine wickets at an average of 16.0.

TRIVIA ANSWER: Garfield Sobers was a joint Australia-Barbados citizen when he was knighted in 1980. He acquired Australian citizenship when he married Australian Prue Kirby in September 1969. They had two sons, Matthew and Daniel, and a daughter, Genevieve. The couple divorced in 1990. Sir Garfield also was a talented golfer having represented Barbados.